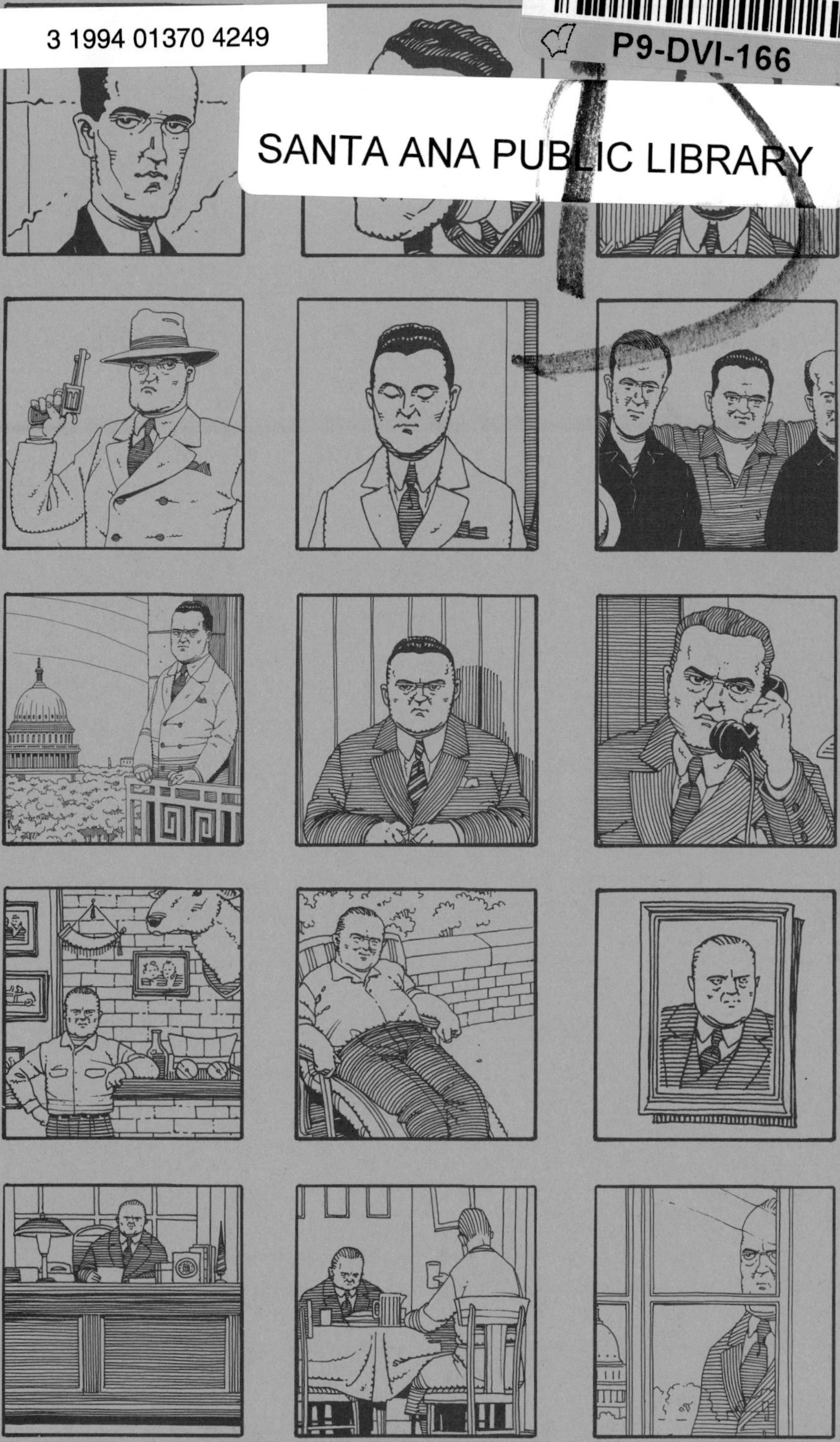

1/08

J. EDGAR HOOVER

J. EDGAR HOOVER

A GRAPHIC BIOGRAPHY by Rick Geary

A NOVEL GRAPHIC from HILL AND WANG

A division of FARRAR, STRAUS AND GIROUX NEW YORK

HILL AND WANG
A division of Farrar, Straus and Giroux
18 West 18th Street, New York 10011

Serious Comics GNC, LLC
621 East 11th Street, New York 10009

Library of Congress Cataloging-in-Publication Data
Geary, Rick.
    J. Edgar Hoover : a graphic biography / text and art by Rick Geary. — 1st ed.
      p. cm.
    ISBN-13: 978-0-8090-9503-2 (hardcover : alk. paper)
    ISBN-10: 0-8090-9503-3 (hardcover : alk. paper)
    1. Hoover, J. Edgar (John Edgar), 1895–1972—Comic books, strips, etc. 2. United States—Federal Bureau of Investigation—Officials and employees—Biography—Comic books, strips, etc. 3. Police—United States—Biography—Comic books, strips, etc. 4. Government executives—United States—Biography—Comic books, strips, etc. I. Title.
HV7911.H6H45 2008
363.25092—dc22
[B]

2007025193

Produced by Jessica Marshall, Ph.D., and Andrew J. Helfer
Lettering by Dan Nakrosis

www.fsgbooks.com
www.seriouscomics.com

1 3 5 7 9 10 8 6 4 2

J. EDGAR HOOVER

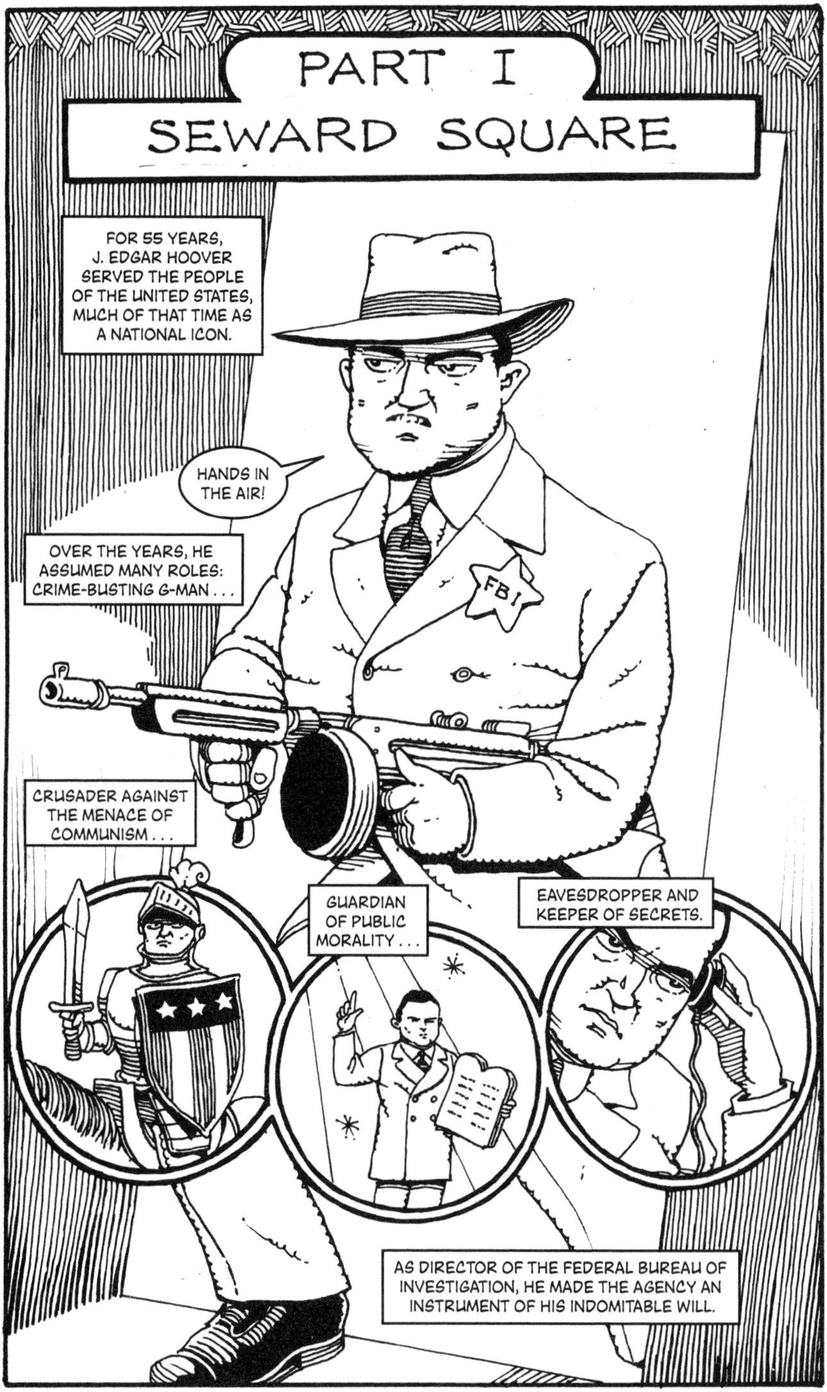
PART I
SEWARD SQUARE
FOR 55 YEARS, J. EDGAR HOOVER SERVED THE PEOPLE OF THE UNITED STATES, MUCH OF THAT TIME AS A NATIONAL ICON.
HANDS IN THE AIR!
OVER THE YEARS, HE ASSUMED MANY ROLES: CRIME-BUSTING G-MAN . . .
FBI
CRUSADER AGAINST THE MENACE OF COMMUNISM . . .
GUARDIAN OF PUBLIC MORALITY . . .
EAVESDROPPER AND KEEPER OF SECRETS.
AS DIRECTOR OF THE FEDERAL BUREAU OF INVESTIGATION, HE MADE THE AGENCY AN INSTRUMENT OF HIS INDOMITABLE WILL.

HE WAS A LIFELONG RESIDENT OF THE NATION'S CAPITAL AND WATCHED IT GROW FROM THE QUIET, TRADITION-BOUND SOUTHERN TOWN OF HIS YOUTH...

...TO THE SPRAWLING CENTER OF POWER IT REMAINS TO THIS DAY.

OUT NOW

MANY OF THESE CHANGES HE HELPED TO BRING ABOUT HIMSELF, AS HE BECAME ONE OF THE MOST POWERFUL, ADMIRED—AND FEARED—MEN OF HIS TIME.

YET HIS ORIGINS WERE LITTLE DIFFERENT FROM THOSE OF MOST AMERICANS.

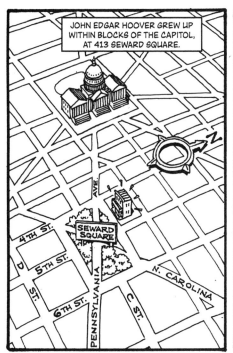

JOHN EDGAR HOOVER GREW UP WITHIN BLOCKS OF THE CAPITOL, AT 413 SEWARD SQUARE.

SEWARD SQUARE

4TH ST.

5TH ST.

6TH ST.

D ST.

C ST.

N. CAROLINA

PENNSYLVANIA AVE.

IT WAS A TREE-LINED, MIDDLE-INCOME NEIGHBORHOOD, HOME TO WASHINGTON'S BURGEONING CLASS OF GOVERNMENT WORKERS.

HE CAME INTO THE WORLD IN AN UPSTAIRS BEDROOM ON JANUARY 1, 1895.

THE YOUNGEST CHILD OF DICKERSON HOOVER, AGE 38, AND ANNIE SHEITLIN HOOVER, AGE 34.

HIS OLDER SIBLINGS: DICKERSON JR. (BORN 1880) AND LILLIAN (BORN 1882).

ANOTHER SISTER, SADIE, DIED OF DIPHTHERIA IN 1893, AT AGE 3.

EDGAR WAS THE ADORED AND DOTED-UPON "REPLACEMENT" CHILD.

HE ATTENDED THE NEARBY BRENT ELEMENTARY SCHOOL, AND AT AGE 11 PUBLISHED A NEIGHBORHOOD NEWSPAPER, THE *WEEKLY REVIEW*.

IN IT HE CHRONICLED THE DOINGS OF HIS FAMILY, THE PEOPLE HE KNEW, AND EVENTS IN THE WORLD AT LARGE— INCLUDING REPORTS OF CRIMES BOTH LOCAL AND NATIONAL.

DURING THESE YEARS, HE ACQUIRED THE NICKNAME "SPEED." TWO STORIES EXPLAIN ITS ORIGIN. ONE IS FROM HIS EARLIEST JOB, CARRYING PEOPLE'S GROCERIES HOME FROM A NEARBY MARKET, A TASK HE PERFORMED WITH REMARKABLE CELERITY.

THE OTHER IS THAT, TO OVERCOME A YOUTHFUL STAMMER, HE WAS ADVISED TO SPEAK AS QUICKLY AS POSSIBLE— AN INCLINATION THAT STAYED WITH HIM THROUGHOUT HIS LIFE.

AT CENTRAL HIGH SCHOOL, YOUNG EDGAR CAME INTO HIS OWN AS A TIRELESS WORKER AND HIGH ACHIEVER.

HIS COMBATIVE SPIRIT WAS NURTURED IN THE SCHOOL'S DEBATING SOCIETY . . .

. . . WHILE HIS PASSION FOR ORDER AND DISCIPLINE RECEIVED ITS OUTLET IN THE CADET CORPS.

ON WEEKENDS HE TAUGHT SUNDAY SCHOOL—WITH HIS OLDER BROTHER, "DICK"—AT THE OLD FIRST PRESBYTERIAN CHURCH . . .

. . . A REFLECTION OF HIS DEEP BELIEF IN THE TRADITIONAL MORAL ORDER . . . THE WHITE CHRISTIAN VISION OF GOOD VERSUS EVIL.

ALTHOUGH ACTIVE AND OUTGOING, "SPEED" HOOVER HAD FEW MALE FRIENDS, AND CERTAINLY NO GIRLFRIENDS.

A SERIOUS LAD, HE WAS DEVOTED TO HIS FAMILY ABOVE ALL.

7

IN 1913, AS THE NEW PRESIDENT, WOODROW WILSON, BEGAN HIS TERM OF OFFICE, EDGAR GRADUATED FROM CENTRAL HIGH.

IN OCTOBER OF THAT YEAR, HE ENTERED GEORGE WASHINGTON UNIVERSITY, WITH THE GOAL OF A DEGREE IN LAW.

TO FINANCE HIS EDUCATION, HE FOUND A JOB AT THE LIBRARY OF CONGRESS, AS A JUNIOR MESSENGER.

HE JOINED THE KAPPA ALPHA FRATERNITY.

IN THE SPRING OF 1916, HE RECEIVED HIS BACHELOR OF LAW DEGREE.

HE CONTINUED AT THE UNIVERSITY FOR ANOTHER YEAR TO EARN HIS MASTER'S DEGREE, AND PASSED THE BAR EXAM IN JUNE 1917.

HE WAS NEVER TO BECOME A PRACTICING ATTORNEY, HOWEVER, AS UNFORESEEN EVENTS IN HOOVER'S PERSONAL LIFE INTERVENED, EVEN AS THE NATION EDGED CLOSER TO ENTERING THE GREAT WAR IN EUROPE.

DICKERSON HOOVER, SR., A MAP MAKER FOR THE DEPARTMENT OF THE INTERIOR, LEFT HIS JOB, AT AGE 60, AFTER PERIODS OF SEVERE MENTAL STRAIN AND DEPRESSION.

HE WOULD BE IN AND OUT OF ASYLUMS FOR THE REMAINDER OF HIS LIFE.

SINCE HIS BROTHER AND SISTER NOW HAD FAMILIES OF THEIR OWN, IT FELL TO EDGAR TO BE "MAN OF THE HOUSE."

HE WAS NOW HIS MOTHER'S PROTECTOR AND BREADWINNER.

ON APRIL 2, 1917, THE PRESIDENT ASKED CONGRESS TO DECLARE WAR ON GERMANY.

THE DAY HAS COME WHEN AMERICA IS PRIVILEGED TO SPEND HER BLOOD AND HER MIGHT FOR THE PRINCIPLES THAT GAVE HER BIRTH . . .

AND THE NATION ENTERED AN UNPRECEDENTED WORLDWIDE CONFLICT.

ON JULY 26, THE 22-YEAR-OLD JOHN EDGAR HOOVER ENTERED A MAKESHIFT OFFICE IN AN ANNEX OF THE RAPIDLY EXPANDING DEPARTMENT OF JUSTICE, HAVING ACCEPTED A POST OBTAINED FOR HIM BY HIS MOTHER'S COUSIN, A FEDERAL JUDGE.

IN ADDITION TO HIS FATHER AND UNCLE, A GRANDFATHER, A COUSIN, AND HIS OLDER BROTHER WERE WORKERS IN THE FEDERAL BUREAUCRACY—THE "FAMILY BUSINESS."

9

UNDER ATTORNEY GENERAL THOMAS GREGORY, EDGAR WORKED FOR THE NEWLY FORMED ALIEN ENEMY REGISTRATION SECTION, WITHIN THE DEPARTMENT'S WAR EMERGENCY DIVISION . . .

. . . A POSITION THAT OFFERED DEFERMENT FROM THE DRAFT.

HIS JOB WAS TO TRACK AND REGISTER GERMAN AND AUSTRO-HUNGARIAN NATIONALS WITHIN THE UNITED STATES, AND IN IT HE DEVELOPED THE SKILLS THAT WOULD SUSTAIN HIM FOR A LIFETIME . . .

. . . THE PROCESSING OF INTELLIGENCE, THE ORGANIZING OF FILES AND RECORDS, THE SCRUTINY OF PEOPLE'S PERSONAL LIVES.

AS AMERICAN BOYS WENT OVERSEAS TO FIGHT, THE NATION WAS IN A PANIC OVER SPIES, TRAITORS, AND SABOTEURS.

THE YOUNG MAN PROVED SO ADEPT AT HIS JOB THAT HE WAS SOON ELEVATED TO THE POST OF SPECIAL ATTORNEY . . .

. . . AND IN 1918 HE WAS ALLOWED TO HIRE A SECRETARY, A YOUNG WOMAN NAMED HELEN GANDY, WHO WOULD REMAIN A TRUSTED ASSISTANT FOR HIS ENTIRE CAREER.

PART II
THE RED HUNTER

IN THE FALL OF 1917, AS AMERICA REMAINED IMMERSED IN THE GREAT WAR, THE NEW GOVERNMENT OF RUSSIA—WHICH HAD OUSTED THE TSAR AND HIS AUTOCRACY THE PREVIOUS FEBRUARY—WAS ITSELF TAKEN OVER BY THE COMMUNIST BOLSHEVIK FACTION.

THE STAGE WAS SET FOR A CONFLICT THAT WOULD LAST THROUGHOUT THE CENTURY— ONE IN WHICH J. EDGAR HOOVER (AS HE NOW SIGNED HIS NAME) WOULD PLAY A CENTRAL ROLE.

WITH THE END OF THE WAR, IN NOVEMBER 1918, MUCH OF EUROPE FELL INTO CHAOS. MANY NATIONS SEEMED ON THE BRINK OF A COMMUNIST TAKEOVER SIMILAR TO RUSSIA'S.

WORLDWIDE REVOLUTION WAS THE COMMUNIST CALL OF THE DAY.

IN AMERICA, THE FEAR OF GERMAN SUBVERSION WAS REPLACED BY A FULL-BLOWN RED SCARE.

A. MITCHELL PALMER, THE NEW ATTORNEY GENERAL, WAS A DEDICATED ANTI-COMMUNIST.

THE MORE SO AFTER HIS HOME WAS DESTROYED BY AN ANARCHIST BOMB IN JUNE 1919.

PALMER ASKED HOOVER TO REMAIN IN THE JUSTICE DEPARTMENT AS HIS SPECIAL ASSISTANT, HEADING THE NEW "RADICAL" DIVISION . . .

. . . A POST TO WHICH THE YOUNG MAN BROUGHT UNIQUE SKILLS.

TO HOOVER, COMMUNISM WAS A PERNICIOUS ORTHODOXY TOTALLY ALIEN IN ITS ORIGIN.

ITS PROPONENTS WERE FOREIGNERS OUT TO UPROOT AMERICAN VALUES.

WITH THE FERVOR OF A CHAMPION DEBATER, HE EDUCATED HIMSELF TO BECOME AN AUTHORITY ON RADICAL ACTIVITY AT HOME AND ABROAD.

HIS CARD CATALOG GREW TO 200,000 ENTRIES, NOT MERELY OF COMMUNISTS BUT ALSO OF LIBERAL ACTIVISTS AND SOCIAL PROGRESSIVES— ANYONE, IN FACT, WHO HAD EXPRESSED DISSENT.

THE WIRY AND ENERGETIC 24-YEAR-OLD IMPRESSED HIS SUPERIORS WITH HIS EFFICIENCY, HIS RELIABILITY, HIS HIGH MORAL CHARACTER, AND HIS ABSOLUTE LACK OF SELF-DOUBT.

IN 1920 HE JOINED THE FREEMASONS, AN ORGANIZATION WITH WHICH HE SHARED A BELIEF IN WHAT THEY CALLED "100% AMERICANISM."

IN OCTOBER 1919, HE HIRED A YOUNG MAN NAMED FRANK BAUGHMAN AS HIS ASSISTANT, AND THEY BECAME INSEPARABLE COMPANIONS.

THE DASHING AND SOCIALLY OUTGOING BAUGHMAN WAS THE FIRST OF HOOVER'S SEVERAL PROTÉGÉS AND FAVORITES.

HOOVER AND BAUGHMAN WERE DEDICATED TO THEIR WORK AND KEPT A BUSTLING OFFICE.

THEY COORDINATED WITH THE DEPARTMENT OF LABOR TO ARRANGE FOR THE IDENTIFICATION AND DEPORTATION OF THOUSANDS OF IMMIGRANTS.

THE RAIDS OF NOVEMBER 1919 LED TO THE ARREST OF MORE THAN 600 MEMBERS OF THE UNION OF RUSSIAN WORKERS.

DEPORTATION WAS DEEMED AN "ADMINISTRATIVE ACTION," NOT A PUNISHMENT. THUS, HOOVER COULD BYPASS THE COURTS AND THE ORDINARY CONSTITUTIONAL SAFEGUARDS—SUCH AS HABEAS CORPUS AND A RIGHT TO COUNSEL.

REALIZING THE VALUE OF PUBLICITY, HE SOUGHT TO GIVE A FACE TO THE COMMUNIST THREAT BY NETTING A "BIG FISH."

THIS CAME IN THE PERSON OF EMMA GOLDMAN, THE NOTORIOUS ANARCHIST AND FREE-LOVE ADVOCATE—WHO HAD BEEN A U.S. RESIDENT FOR 34 YEARS. TO HOOVER, SHE REPRESENTED EVERYTHING VILE.

ON DECEMBER 21, 1919, MEMBERS OF THE PRESS GATHERED AT A PIER IN LOWER NEW YORK TO WITNESS THE SAILING OF THE USS *BUFORD*—MEANT TO BE THE FIRST OF MANY "SOVIET ARKS."

ON BOARD WERE GOLDMAN AND MORE THAN 200 OTHER RADICALS, BOUND FOR RUSSIA.

AFTER THIS, HIS FIRST BIG MEDIA PRODUCTION, THE YOUNG MAN BEGAN KEEPING A BOOK OF HIS PRESS CLIPPINGS.

TO MANY, HOWEVER, THE ATTORNEY GENERAL AND HIS SPECIAL ASSISTANT OVERSTEPPED THEIR BOUNDS WITH THE INFAMOUS PALMER RAIDS OF JANUARY 2, 1920.

WITH GREAT PRESS FANFARE, AS MANY AS 6,000 IMMIGRANTS WERE ROUNDED UP IN DOZENS OF CITIES AND PUT INTO DETENTION CAMPS.

IN BOSTON, THE PRISONERS WERE CHAINED TOGETHER AND PARADED THROUGH THE STREETS.

IN DETROIT, THEY WERE DETAINED IN A WINDOWLESS CORRIDOR WITH NO TOILET FACILITIES.

15

OF 6,328 WARRANTS ISSUED, 4,000 ACTUAL ARRESTS WERE MADE, AND FROM THEM JUST 1,000 DEPORTATIONS ORDERED.

BUT THESE DEPORTATIONS WERE NEVER TO TAKE PLACE.

PALMER, WHO HAD BEEN HOPING TO RUN FOR PRESIDENT, AND HIS RED HUNTERS BEGAN TO LOSE THE SUPPORT OF BOTH CONGRESS AND THE PUBLIC.

THE DEPARTMENT OF LABOR DECLARED THAT ALIEN RESIDENTS HAD THE RIGHT TO COUNSEL IN DEPORTATION PROCEEDINGS.

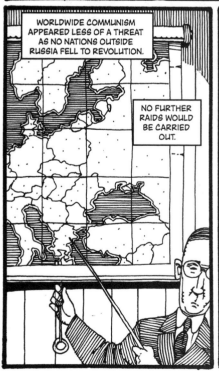

WORLDWIDE COMMUNISM APPEARED LESS OF A THREAT AS NO NATIONS OUTSIDE RUSSIA FELL TO REVOLUTION.

NO FURTHER RAIDS WOULD BE CARRIED OUT.

BUT TO J. EDGAR HOOVER, COMMUNISM REMAINED THE PRIME EVIL OF THE AGE, NOT MERELY A POLITICAL PHILOSOPHY BUT A MALIGNANT WAY OF LIFE THAT UNDERMINED DECENT SOCIETY.

IN MARCH 1921, A NEW PRESIDENT, WARREN G. HARDING, TOOK OFFICE.

THE PRESIDENT'S OHIO CRONY HARRY DAUGHERTY BECAME ATTORNEY GENERAL...

...AND TO HEAD THE JUSTICE DEPARTMENT'S BUREAU OF INVESTIGATION, DAUGHERTY CHOSE ANOTHER OHIO FRIEND, THE WELL-KNOWN DETECTIVE WILLIAM J. BURNS.

HOOVER BECAME BURNS'S ASSISTANT DIRECTOR.

IN THE FIRST OF MANY INSTANCES, HIS CAREFUL NONPARTISAN STANCE ENABLED HIM TO REMAIN IN GOVERNMENT SERVICE NO MATTER WHICH PARTY WAS IN POWER.

BUREAU OF INVESTIGATION

DURING THESE YEARS, HOOVER KEPT A LOW PUBLIC PROFILE, WHILE REMAINING INDISPENSABLE TO HIS SUPERIORS.

THE BUREAU, AFTER ALL, HAD LITTLE JURISDICTION OUTSIDE OF A SMALL NUMBER OF INTERSTATE CRIMES.

17

IN 1922, DICKERSON HOOVER DIED FROM THE EFFECTS OF HIS LINGERING DEPRESSION . . .

. . . AND ANNIE HOOVER'S YOUNGEST CHILD CONTINUED TO LIVE WITH HER IN THE HOUSE ON SEWARD SQUARE.

THE FOLLOWING YEAR, THE TROUBLED HARDING ADMINISTRATION CAME TO AN END WITH THE SUDDEN DEATH OF THE PRESIDENT.

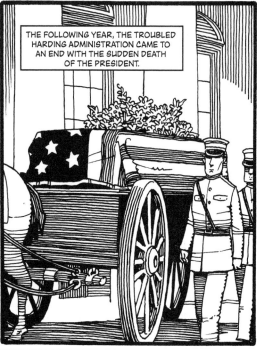

CALVIN COOLIDGE WAS ELEVATED TO THE PRESIDENCY, JUST AS SEVERAL CORRUPTION SCANDALS BECAME PUBLIC KNOWLEDGE.

IN THE TEAPOT DOME AFFAIR, SECRETARY OF THE INTERIOR ALBERT B. FALL WAS ACCUSED OF SECRETLY SELLING THE NAVY'S OIL LANDS FOR PERSONAL PROFIT.

THE JUSTICE DEPARTMENT, PARTICULARLY THE BUREAU OF INVESTIGATION, WAS ACCUSED OF COMPLICITY.

BOTH DAUGHERTY AND BURNS WERE FORCED TO RESIGN THEIR OFFICES . . .

. . . CLEARING THE WAY FOR THE RISE OF J. EDGAR HOOVER, WHO HAD AGAIN MANAGED TO AVOID ANY CONNECTION TO THE MISDEEDS OF THOSE IN POWER ABOVE HIM.

PART III

SCIENTIFIC CRIME DETECTION

ON MAY 10, 1924, A DATE THAT WOULD BE MEMORIZED AND MEMORIALIZED IN THE YEARS TO COME, J. EDGAR HOOVER WAS CALLED INTO THE OFFICE OF THE NEW ATTORNEY GENERAL, HARLAN F. STONE . . .

. . . AND APPOINTED, AT AGE 29, ACTING—AND SOON THE OFFICIAL—DIRECTOR OF THE BUREAU OF INVESTIGATION.

1924
10
MAY
SATURDAY

THE BUREAU WAS STILL A RATHER SMALL AND INEFFECTUAL ARM OF THE GOVERNMENT . . .

. . . A REPOSITORY FOR POLITICAL PATRONAGE, SUBJECT TO CORRUPTION OF ALL KINDS.

CONGRESS SAW THE BUREAU, ESTABLISHED IN 1908 UNDER PRESIDENT THEODORE ROOSEVELT, ONLY AS AN ARM OF PRESIDENTIAL AMBITION.

AGENTS WERE NOT EMPOWERED TO CARRY FIREARMS OR MAKE ARRESTS.

THEY CONFINED THEIR ACTIVITIES PRIMARILY TO STRIKEBREAKING . . .

. . . AND TO ENFORCING THE MANN ACT, AN ANTIPROSTITUTION LAW THAT FORBADE THE TRANSPORTING OF WOMEN ACROSS STATE LINES FOR IMMORAL PURPOSES.

HOOVER ASKED FOR AND RECEIVED COMPLETE AUTONOMY . . .

. . . AND THE AUTHORITY TO "CLEAN HOUSE" IN THE WAY HE SAW FIT.

HE SET OUT TO MAKE THE BUREAU A MODEL OF PROGRESSIVE EFFICIENCY.

THE BUREAU MUST BE DIVORCED FROM POLITICS AND NOT BE A CATCHALL FOR POLITICAL HACKS. APPOINTMENTS MUST BE BASED ON MERIT. PROMOTIONS WILL BE MADE ONLY ON PROVEN ABILITY. AND THE BUREAU WILL BE RESPONSIBLE ONLY TO THE ATTORNEY GENERAL.

IN SHORT ORDER, HE DRASTICALLY STREAMLINED BUREAU PERSONNEL...

...FIRING ALL POLITICAL APPOINTEES, "INCOMPETENTS, AND TIME-SERVERS."

HE DIVIDED THE BUREAU'S OPERATIONS INTO SIX MAJOR DIVISIONS...

...INCLUDING A DIVISION OF IDENTIFICATION, WHICH COORDINATED ALL FILES ON SUSPECT INDIVIDUALS IN ONE PLACE.

NEWLY HIRED AGENTS WERE EXPECTED TO BE OF THE HIGHEST CHARACTER AND ABILITY.

ALL WERE REQUIRED TO HAVE HAD TRAINING IN THE LAW OR ACCOUNTING.

THE DIRECTOR DISCOURAGED DRINKING, SMOKING, AND WOMANIZING.

HE SOUGHT TO ESTABLISH A SYSTEM OF TOTAL CONTROL OVER THE BUREAU'S 53 FIELD OFFICES . . .

. . . WITH REGULAR INSPECTIONS AND DETAILED REPORTS FROM THE AGENTS IN CHARGE.

DURING THESE EARLY YEARS, HOOVER ENDEAVORED TO GIVE THE BUREAU A PREDOMINANTLY WHITE, MALE, AND PROTESTANT IMAGE.

FEW BLACKS, WOMEN, JEWS, OR FOREIGNERS WERE HIRED. POLITICAL LIBERALS WERE FROWNED UPON.

THE NEW BUREAU WAS TO EMBODY THE LATEST DEVELOPMENTS IN SCIENTIFIC CRIME DETECTION.

THE MASSIVE FILE OF FINGERPRINTS CONSOLIDATED COLLECTIONS FROM POLICE ORGANIZATIONS AROUND THE COUNTRY.

BALLISTICS ANALYSIS COULD MATCH A BULLET TO THE GUN THAT FIRED IT.

THE "CRIME LAB" ANALYZED BLOOD AND MICROSCOPIC TRACE EVIDENCE.

EXPERTS WERE TRAINED IN THE SCRUTINY OF HANDWRITING, SHOEPRINTS, TIRE TRACKS.

IN SHORT ORDER, AS MANY PEOPLE OBSERVED, THE BUREAU BECAME OVERQUALIFIED FOR ITS JOB.

OFFICE OF THE DIRECTOR

PENDING NEW FEDERAL LEGISLATION, MOST CRIMES REMAINED THE PROBLEM OF LOCAL COMMUNITIES.

IN 1925, AS A SERVICE TO THE PRESIDENT, HOOVER BEGAN PROVIDING INTELLIGENCE ON POLITICIANS AND POLITICAL GROUPS, ALLIES AS WELL AS ADVERSARIES . . .

. . . A SIDELINE TO CRIMINAL INVESTIGATION THAT HE WOULD BE CALLED UPON TO CONTINUE THROUGHOUT HIS CAREER.

EVER MINDFUL OF PUBLIC RELATIONS, HE ESTABLISHED THE CRIME RECORDS DIVISION, TO PROVIDE NATIONAL STATISTICS ON CRIME TO LOCAL GOVERNMENTS AND POLICE FORCES.

UNIFORM CRIME REPORTS

BEFORE LONG, IT BECAME THE BUREAU'S PROPAGANDA ARM, WITH THE JOB OF KEEPING THE BUREAU IN THE PUBLIC EYE.

THE WRITER REX COLLIER, AT THE WASHINGTON STAR, PROVIDED A SERIES OF FAVORABLE ARTICLES.

HE DESCRIBED THE DIRECTOR AS "UNCLE SAM'S BOYISH-LOOKING SHERLOCK HOLMES."

OVER THE 1920S, HOOVER GRADUALLY LOST HIS BOYISH LOOK, DEVELOPING THE BEEFY "BULLDOG" PHYSIQUE SO FAMILIAR TO THE PUBLIC.

HE FAVORED LINEN SUITS, WITH FASHIONABLE TIES AND ACCESSORIES.

HE CONTINUED TO LIVE WITH HIS MOTHER IN THEIR SEWARD SQUARE HOME.

TWO STRONG PERSONALITIES UNDER ONE ROOF, YET THEY MANAGED.

SHE MADE SURE THAT HIS POACHED EGG ON TOAST WAS PREPARED EACH MORNING TO HIS EXACTING SPECIFICATIONS.

THEIR AIREDALE, SPEE DEE BOZO, THE FIRST IN A LONG LINE OF HOOVER DOGS, WOULD BECOME THE RECIPIENT OF THE BREAKFAST IF IT FAILED TO QUALIFY.

HE BEGAN COLLECTING ORIENTAL ANTIQUES AND CURIOS.

IN 1928, HOOVER HIRED THE MAN WHO WOULD BECOME HIS SECOND-IN-COMMAND AND CLOSEST COMPANION FOR THE REST OF HIS LIFE.

CLYDE TOLSON, AGE 28, WAS, LIKE HOOVER, A HIGH ACHIEVER AND A GRADUATE OF THE GEORGE WASHINGTON UNIVERSITY LAW SCHOOL.

BY THIS TIME, FRANK BAUGHMAN HAD FALLEN OUT OF FAVOR.

THOUGH HE REMAINED IN THE BUREAU, HIS FRIENDSHIP WITH HOOVER COOLED AFTER HE MARRIED AND STARTED A FAMILY.

TOLSON QUICKLY ROSE IN RANK, BECOMING ASSISTANT AND THEN ASSOCIATE DIRECTOR.

HE AND HOOVER RODE TO WORK TOGETHER, SHARED LUNCHES, DINNERS, AND EVENTUALLY, VACATIONS.

THE STOCK MARKET CRASH OF 1929 PLUNGED THE NATION INTO ECONOMIC DEPRESSION. A SENSE OF MALAISE AND DISORDER PREVAILED.

WIDESPREAD POVERTY IGNITED A NATIONWIDE AWARENESS OF CRIME, PARTICULARLY BANK ROBBERY.

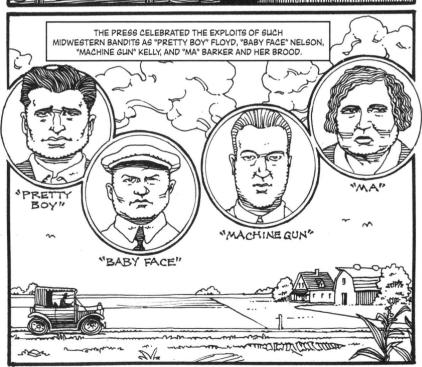

THE PRESS CELEBRATED THE EXPLOITS OF SUCH MIDWESTERN BANDITS AS "PRETTY BOY" FLOYD, "BABY FACE" NELSON, "MACHINE GUN" KELLY, AND "MA" BARKER AND HER BROOD.

"PRETTY BOY"

"BABY FACE"

"MACHINE GUN"

"MA"

POPULAR MOVIES TOLD THE STORIES OF CAREER CRIMINALS . . .

. . . EDWARD G. ROBINSON AS "LITTLE CAESAR," JAMES CAGNEY AS "THE PUBLIC ENEMY."

THE CRIME OF KIDNAPPING WAS ALSO IN ITS HEYDAY . . .

. . . CULMINATING IN THE MARCH 1932 ABDUCTION AND MURDER OF AVIATION HERO CHARLES LINDBERGH'S YOUNG SON.

ALTHOUGH HOOVER POSITIONED HIMSELF AND THE BUREAU FRONT AND CENTER IN THE CASE . . .

. . . THERE WAS LITTLE HE COULD DO UNTIL THE PASSAGE LATER THAT YEAR OF LEGISLATION MAKING KIDNAPPING A FEDERAL OFFENSE.

THE STAGE WAS SET FOR THE EMERGENCE OF A NATIONAL LAW-ENFORCEMENT ENTITY . . .

. . . AND A NEW TYPE OF AMERICAN HERO.

PART IV
G - MEN

THE ELECTION OF FRANKLIN D. ROOSEVELT PROMISED A "NEW DEAL" FOR THE NATION.

THE ONLY THING WE HAVE TO FEAR IS FEAR ITSELF.

THE NEW PRESIDENT AND HIS ATTORNEY GENERAL, HOMER CUMMINGS, VOWED TO MAKE CRIME FIGHTING A TOP PRIORITY. TO THIS END, J. EDGAR HOOVER WAS REAPPOINTED AS DIRECTOR OF THE BUREAU OF INVESTIGATION.

OVER THE NEXT TWO YEARS, SEVERAL INCIDENTS BROUGHT THE BUREAU ONTO THE NATION'S FRONT PAGES.

ON JUNE 17, 1933, BUREAU AGENTS ESCORTING AN ESCAPED CONVICT BACK TO PRISON WERE AMBUSHED BY GANGSTERS IN FRONT OF KANSAS CITY'S UNION STATION.

THE "KANSAS CITY MASSACRE" LEFT ONE AGENT AND THREE LOCAL POLICE OFFICERS DEAD. TWO OTHER AGENTS WERE SERIOUSLY WOUNDED. THE PERPETRATORS GOT AWAY.

TO HOOVER, THIS WAS A DIRECT CHALLENGE.

IF IT'S WAR THEY WANT, IT'S WAR THEY'LL GET.

ON JULY 22, ALBERT BATES, GEORGE "MACHINE GUN" KELLY, AND HIS WIFE, KATHRYN, KIDNAPPED THE OKLAHOMA OILMAN CHARLES URSCHEL . . .

. . . GIVING THE BUREAU ITS FIRST CHANCE TO CRACK A CASE ON THE NATIONAL LEVEL, AND WITH FULL NATIONAL PUBLICITY.

ON SEPTEMBER 26, AFTER THE RANSOM HAD BEEN PAID AND THE VICTIM RELEASED, AGENTS TRACKED THE COUPLE TO A HOUSE IN MEMPHIS, TENNESSEE.

ACCORDING TO LEGEND, UPON SURRENDERING, KELLY GAVE THE BUREAU ITS NICKNAME.

DON'T SHOOT, G-MEN, DON'T SHOOT!

31

1934 SAW THE BUREAU TAKE ON ITS MOST FAMOUS CASE THUS FAR.

THE NOTORIOUS ROBBER JOHN DILLINGER ESCAPED TWICE FROM JAIL AND LED AGENTS ON A CHASE THROUGH SEVERAL STATES.

MELVIN PURVIS, HEAD OF THE CHICAGO FIELD OFFICE—AND A HOOVER PROTÉGÉ—HEADED THE PURSUIT.

PURVIS'S MEN TRACED DILLINGER AND HIS GANG TO A CABIN AT THE LITTLE BOHEMIA RESORT IN NORTHERN WISCONSIN.

THE RAID WAS A SPECTACULAR FAILURE, TURNING INTO A CHAOS OF GUNFIRE . . .

. . . IN WHICH A BUREAU AGENT AND A BYSTANDER WERE KILLED. THE OUTLAWS ESCAPED UNHARMED.

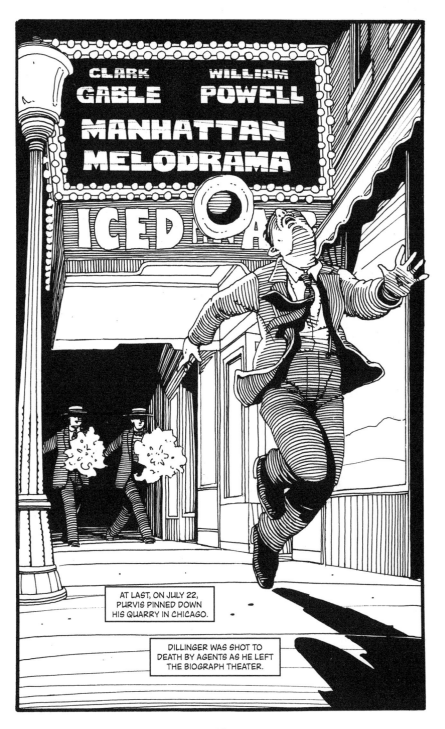

CLARK GABLE WILLIAM POWELL

MANHATTAN MELODRAMA

AT LAST, ON JULY 22, PURVIS PINNED DOWN HIS QUARRY IN CHICAGO.

DILLINGER WAS SHOT TO DEATH BY AGENTS AS HE LEFT THE BIOGRAPH THEATER.

THE BUREAU GAINED NATIONAL ATTENTION AS NEVER BEFORE. FOR MANY YEARS, HOOVER DISPLAYED A COLLECTION OF DILLINGER RELICS IN THE ANTEROOM TO HIS OFFICE.

CHICAGO

PUBLIC ENEMY NUMBER ONE!
$20,000 REWARD!

ALTHOUGH THE ELIMINATION OF DILLINGER WAS THE RESULT OF AN INFORMANT'S TIP, THE DIRECTOR PREFERRED TO EXPLAIN THAT IT CAME ABOUT THROUGH THE BUREAU'S SCIENTIFIC DETECTION METHODS.

IN SEPTEMBER, HOOVER POSED WITH NEW YORK CITY POLICE OFFICERS AFTER THE ARREST OF BRUNO RICHARD HAUPTMANN FOR THE KIDNAPPING AND MURDER OF THE LINDBERGH CHILD . . .

. . . ALTHOUGH THE BUREAU'S PART IN HIS CAPTURE WAS MINIMAL.

HAUPTMANN

IN OCTOBER 1934, MELVIN PURVIS AND HIS MEN TRACKED DOWN AND KILLED CHARLES "PRETTY BOY" FLOYD IN AN OHIO CORNFIELD . . .

. . . BRINGING FURTHER GLORY TO HIMSELF AND THE BUREAU.

THE TITLE OF PUBLIC ENEMY NO. 1 THEN FELL TO GEORGE "BABY FACE" NELSON. PURVIS VOWED TO BRING HIM TO JUSTICE.

NELSON WAS FELLED BY AGENTS IN RURAL ILLINOIS IN NOVEMBER 1934.

34

PURVIS WAS NOW A MEDIA CELEBRITY IN HIS OWN RIGHT, DRAWING THE IRE OF HIS BOSS AND FORMER MENTOR . . .

. . . WHO BELIEVED THE BUREAU SHOULD BE RUN AS A TEAM, WITH NO SINGLE PLAYER STANDING OUT— EXCEPT PERHAPS THE DIRECTOR.

THE AGENT FOUND HIMSELF THE SUBJECT OF NEGATIVE REPORTS AND UNFOUNDED ACCUSATIONS . . .

. . . AND SUCH HARRASSMENT THAT HE RESIGNED FROM THE BUREAU IN JULY 1935.

IN FUTURE YEARS, ANY JOB THAT PURVIS APPLIED FOR WOULD BE OPPOSED BY A DAMAGING REPORT FROM HIS FORMER EMPLOYER.

Star.

MANHUNT
EN CAPTURED

IN THE OFFICIAL HISTORIES OF THE BUREAU, HIS NAME WOULD NEVER BE MENTIONED.

IN 1960, HE WOULD COMMIT SUICIDE . . .

. . . USING THE SAME PISTOL, IT WAS SAID, THAT HE USED IN THE PURSUIT OF JOHN DILLINGER.

AFTER THE EXIT OF PURVIS, THE BUREAU CONTINUED TO KEEP ITS EXPLOITS BEFORE THE PUBLIC.

ON JANUARY 16, 1935, AGENTS KILLED KATE "MA" BARKER AND HER SON FRED IN A FLORIDA SHOOTOUT.

THAT SUMMER, THE BUREAU WAS OFFICIALLY DESIGNATED THE FEDERAL BUREAU OF INVESTIGATION. IT WAS NOW THE FBI.

DEPARTMENT OF JUSTICE
FEDERAL BUREAU OF INVESTIGATION
FIDELITY BRAVERY INTEGRITY

AND J. EDGAR HOOVER WAS NOW THE NATION'S LEADING ANTICRIME SPOKESMAN.

THERE IS NO ROMANCE IN CRIME AND THERE IS NO ROMANCE IN CRIMINALS. THEY ARE RATS, VERMIN, REGURGITATING THEIR FILTH TO DESPOIL THE CLEAN PICTURE OF AMERICAN MANHOOD AND WOMANHOOD.

EACH YEAR THE DIRECTOR WAS OBLIGED TO APPEAR BEFORE CONGRESS TO JUSTIFY THE TAX MONEY SPENT BY THE BUREAU.

IS IT TRUE, DIRECTOR HOOVER, THAT YOU HAVE NEVER PERSONALLY APPREHENDED A CRIMINAL?

Senator

Sen

AT A MEETING IN MARCH 1936, HE WAS ASKED BY A SENATOR WHY HE WAS NOT OUT IN THE FIELD "RISKING HIS NECK" ALONG WITH HIS MEN.

TO HOOVER, THIS WAS A PERSONAL AFFRONT.

ACCORDINGLY, HE FLEW TO NEW ORLEANS IN APRIL TO OVERSEE THE CAPTURE OF ALVIN "CREEPY" KARPIS, A FORMER MEMBER OF MA BARKER'S GANG.

PUT THE CUFFS ON HIM, BOYS!

IN MAY, HOOVER LED A PREDAWN RAID IN TOLEDO, OHIO, TO SEIZE HARRY CAMPBELL, ANOTHER FUGITIVE FROM THE BARKER GANG.

AND IN DECEMBER, HE COMMANDED A SHOOTOUT IN NEW YORK CITY THAT ENDED IN THE CAPTURE OF THE BANK ROBBER HARRY BRUNETTE.

THE DIRECTOR WAS NOW POISED TO BECOME NOT ONLY AMERICA'S LEADING MORAL AUTHORITY, BUT ITS ACTION HERO AS WELL.

PART V
A HOUSEHOLD NAME

ALTHOUGH THEY DIFFERED VASTLY IN POLITICS AND TEMPERAMENT, J. EDGAR HOOVER AND FRANKLIN D. ROOSEVELT WORKED WELL TOGETHER AND SHARED A WARY ADMIRATION.

EACH NEEDED THE OTHER TO ACHIEVE HIS GOALS.

AUGUST 1936: IN A SECRET VERBAL DIRECTIVE, THE PRESIDENT GRANTED HOOVER THE BROAD AND UNLIMITED (AND MOST LIKELY UNCONSTITUTIONAL) AUTHORITY TO CONDUCT SURVEILLANCE UPON AMERICAN CITIZENS.

THIS PROVIDED THE BASIS FOR FORTY YEARS OF BUREAU ACTIVITY.

THEY MONITORED THE MOVEMENTS OF DOMESTIC NAZIS AS WELL AS COMMUNISTS . . .

UNIONS AND UNION LEADERS . . .

STRIK

ANYONE DEEMED BY THE PRESIDENT TO BE A POLITICAL ENEMY.

KANSA

OPLE

MASSACHUSETTS

OTA

MANY NEW AGENTS WERE HIRED DURING THESE YEARS. THEIR NUMBER GREW FROM 1,000 TO 4,000.

BOTH HOOVER AND ROOSEVELT KNEW THE BENEFITS OF A STRONG PUBLIC IMAGE.

G-MEN

THE FBI COURTED THE MAJOR HOLLYWOOD PRODUCERS, CHIEF AMONG THEM JACK WARNER OF WARNER BROTHERS.

THAT STUDIO PRODUCED *G-MEN*, STARRING JAMES CAGNEY.

IN ADDITION, A *G-MEN* RADIO SERIES RAN FOR 13 EPISODES IN 1935.

A PULP MONTHLY PROVED VERY POPULAR . . .

WAR ON CRIME

FLASH GORDON

. . . AS DID A DAILY COMIC STRIP IN THE NATION'S NEWSPAPERS.

41

LOUIS NICHOLS, AN AGENT SINCE 1934, WAS ELEVATED TO HOOVER'S THIRD-IN-COMMAND AND HEAD OF THE BUREAU'S RESEARCH DIVISION—ITS PUBLIC RELATIONS ARM.

AN EXPERIENCED PUBLICIST AND TROUBLESHOOTER, NICHOLS CULTIVATED FRIENDLY JOURNALISTS AND REPORTERS . . .

THE BETTER TO BURNISH THE HOOVER IMAGE . . .

. . . AND TO KEEP THE BUREAU'S VERSION OF EVENTS AS THE ONLY "OFFICIAL" VERSION.

A SERIES OF ADULATORY STORIES RAN IN *AMERICAN* MAGAZINE . . .

. . . PENNED UNDER THE DIRECTOR'S NAME BY ANOTHER HOOVER CRONY, COURTNEY RYLEY COOPER.

IN 1935 THE DIRECTOR WAS FEATURED ON THE COVER OF *TIME* (THE FIRST OF FOUR IN HIS LIFETIME).

IN THE MEANTIME, THE NATION'S NEW HERO LED A QUIET, ORDERED PRIVATE LIFE.

HE AND TOLSON WOULD ARRIVE AT WORK EARLY AND DEPART LATE, OFTEN WORKING WEEKENDS.

THEY LUNCHED INVARIABLY AT HARVEY'S RESTAURANT ON CONNECTICUT AVENUE, ALWAYS AT THE SAME TABLE.

IN THE WINTER, THEY VACATIONED IN MIAMI . . .

IN THE SUMMER, SOUTHERN CALIFORNIA.

BOTH MEN WERE PASSIONATE AFICIONADOS OF HORSERACING.

43

WHEN IN NEW YORK, HOOVER AND TOLSON BECAME REGULARS AT THE CITY'S MOST FAMOUS NIGHTSPOT, THE STORK CLUB.

THERE, THE DIRECTOR BEFRIENDED THE COLUMNIST WALTER WINCHELL.

THE TWO, OVER THE YEARS, WOULD EXCHANGE INFORMATION TO THEIR MUTUAL BENEFIT.

MANY OBSERVERS AT THE TIME, AND FOR DECADES THEREAFTER, ASSUMED THAT HOOVER AND TOLSON WERE LOVERS...

...ALTHOUGH THERE HAS BEEN NO DIRECT EVIDENCE CONFIRMING THIS.

STILL, THEIR COMPANIONSHIP WAS UNDOUBTEDLY SO INTIMATE AND COMFORTABLE THAT, OVER TIME, IT EMBODIED THE CHARACTERISTICS OF A MARRIAGE.

HOOVER WOULD SAY OF HIS SECOND-IN-COMMAND: "HE IS MY ALTER EGO."

44

HE BRISTLED AT ANY QUESTION OF HIS MANHOOD.

TO HIM, HOMOSEXUALITY WAS LIKE ANY OTHER CRIME, NOT A CONDITION BUT A MORAL FAILING.

IN ANY CASE, HOOVER WAS SAID TO HAVE CLOSE FRIENDSHIPS AT THIS TIME WITH SEVERAL WOMEN . . .

. . . CHIEF AMONG THEM LELA ROGERS, A RIGHT-WING ACTIVIST (AND MOTHER OF THE ACTRESS GINGER ROGERS) . . .

. . . AND THE RISING STARLET DOROTHY LAMOUR.

THE DIRECTOR RESERVED HIS STRONGEST VENOM FOR THOSE WHO EXCUSED CRIMINALS AS VICTIMS OF BAD UPBRINGING OR SOCIAL CONDITIONS.

WE NEED A REBUILDING OF THE FOUNDATIONS WHICH MADE THIS NATION THE GREATEST IN ALL HISTORY, BULWARKS FORMED OF MORE STABLE MATERIALS THAN THOSE OF APATHY, SELFISHNESS, AND INDULGENCE.

THE MAJOR TASK OF SOCIETY TODAY IS TO INSURE THAT LAW AND ORDER SHALL REIGN SUPREME.

45

IN 1938, ANNIE HOOVER DIED IN THE HOUSE ON SEWARD SQUARE.

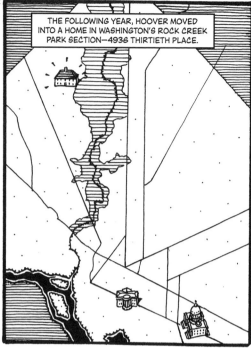

THE FOLLOWING YEAR, HOOVER MOVED INTO A HOME IN WASHINGTON'S ROCK CREEK PARK SECTION—4936 THIRTIETH PLACE.

THERE, HE WOULD LIVE OUT HIS DAYS ALONE, TENDED BY A LIVE-IN COOK AND HOUSEKEEPER.

HE MADE OF THE HOUSE A MEMORIAL TO HIS MOTHER, WITH IMAGES OF HER IN NEARLY EVERY ROOM.

IN SEPTEMBER 1939, GERMANY INVADED POLAND, SETTING OFF THE SECOND WORLD WAR.

AS HITLER SEIZED MORE TERRITORY AND BRITAIN WAS THREATENED, THE U.S. REMAINED OFFICIALLY NEUTRAL.

The Sun

LONDON BOMBED

THE PRESIDENT, HOWEVER, TOOK SECRET STEPS TO PREPARE FOR THE COUNTRY'S DEFENSE.

HE GAVE TO HOOVER AUTHORITY OVER ALL INTELLIGENCE OPERATIONS AGAINST FOREIGN ESPIONAGE WITHIN THE U.S. AND SOUTH AMERICA (WHILE OVERSEAS REMAINED THE PROVINCE OF THE ARMY AND NAVY).

TO THIS END, ROOSEVELT AUTHORIZED TELEPHONE WIRETAPS, ALTHOUGH SUCH ABRIDGMENT OF CIVIL RIGHTS WAS OF QUESTIONABLE LEGALITY.

THE FBI NOW CAME INTO ITS OWN AS THE NATION'S CHIEF ENTITY FOR INTERNAL SECURITY.

THE CUSTODIAL DETENTION PROGRAM WAS INITIATED TO TRACK "DANGEROUS" INDIVIDUALS IN CASE OF WAR.

MORE THAN 13,000 SUBJECTS WERE THUS CATEGORIZED.

IN 1940, AT AGE 45, J. EDGAR HOOVER WAS AT THE TOP OF HIS GAME.

HE CAREFULLY MAINTAINED THE IMPRESSION OF POLITICAL NEUTRALITY. HE BELONGED TO NO PARTY, AND AS A DISTRICT RESIDENT, HE NEVER VOTED.

TO HIS SUPERIORS, HE MERELY PROVIDED RAW INFORMATION, MAKING NO INTERPRETATIONS OR JUDGMENTS.

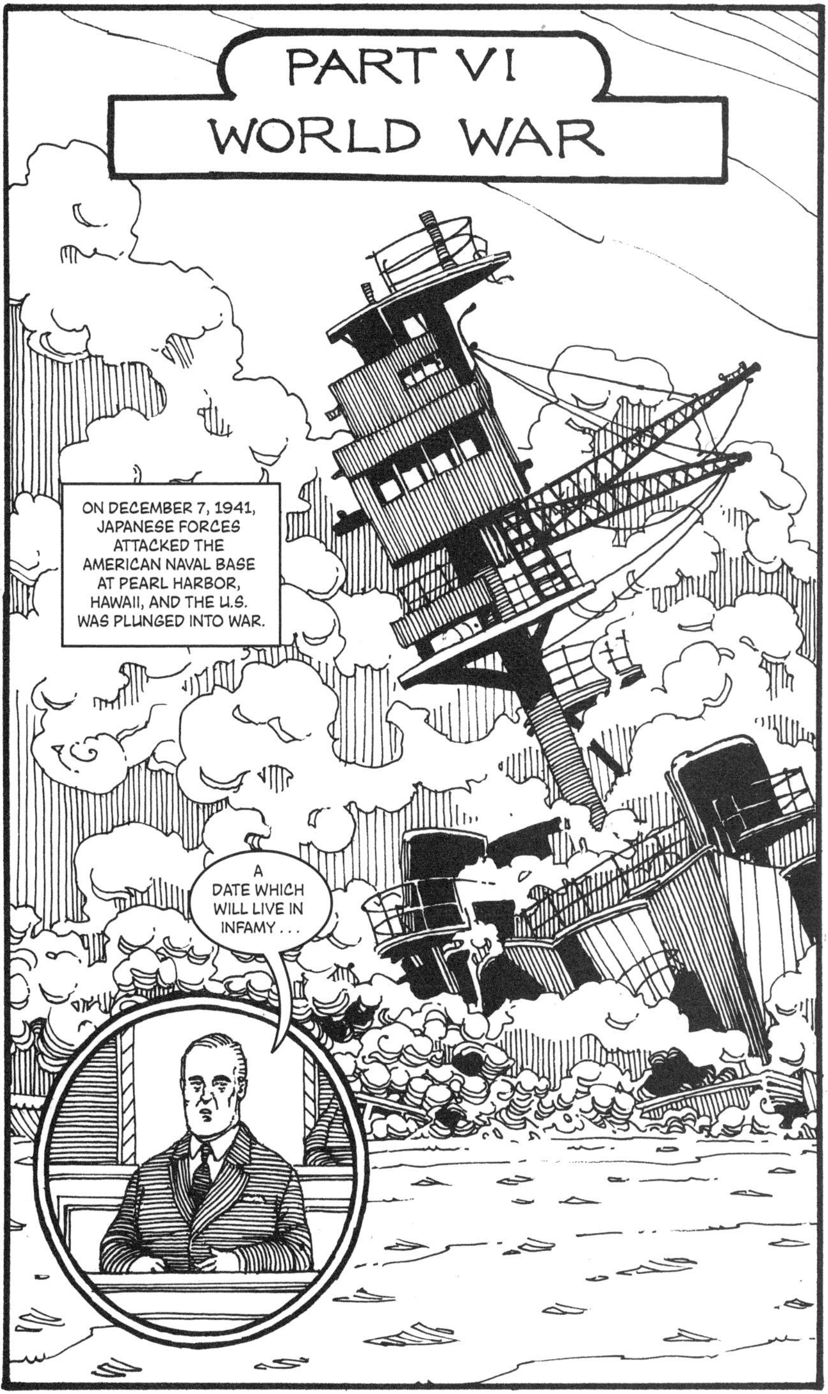
PART VI
WORLD WAR
ON DECEMBER 7, 1941, JAPANESE FORCES ATTACKED THE AMERICAN NAVAL BASE AT PEARL HARBOR, HAWAII, AND THE U.S. WAS PLUNGED INTO WAR.
A DATE WHICH WILL LIVE IN INFAMY . . .

THE ATTACK WAS OBVIOUSLY A MAJOR FAILURE OF INTELLIGENCE. BUT WHOSE?

IN RETROSPECT, SEVERAL KEY PIECES OF INFORMATION HAD BEEN MISINTERPRETED OR IGNORED.

SINCE THE FBI'S INTELLIGENCE-GATHERING PROVINCE DID NOT INCLUDE THE HAWAIIAN ISLANDS, HOOVER WAS CERTAINLY OFF THE HOOK.

HIS DESIRE WAS FOR THE BUREAU TO TAKE OVER ALL INTELLIGENCE GATHERING FOR THE WAR, FOREIGN AS WELL AS DOMESTIC...

...BUT THE PRESIDENT THOUGHT DIFFERENTLY.

OF STRATEGIC SERVICES

OSS

IN 1942, HE AUTHORIZED THE CREATION OF AN INDEPENDENT INTELLIGENCE AGENCY, THE OFFICE OF STRATEGIC SERVICES, OR OSS...

...HEADED BY THE ASSISTANT ATTORNEY GENERAL AND WAR HERO WILLIAM J. "WILD BILL" DONOVAN.

A RESENTFUL HOOVER WOULD TAKE EVERY OPPORTUNITY TO OBSTRUCT THE WORK OF THIS NEW ORGANIZATION.

THE NATION'S TOP CRIME FIGHTER DONNED A NEW IMAGE AS TRACKER OF SPIES AND SABOTEURS.

LEAVE IT TO THE FBI!

CITIZENS COULD BE AT EASE, THE BUREAU WAS IN CONTROL!

HOLLYWOOD FOLLOWED SUIT, WITH SUCH MOVIES AS *THE HOUSE ON 92ND STREET* . . .

NOW PLAYING

THE HOUSE ON 92ND STREET

. . . AND THE RADIO PROGRAM *THIS IS YOUR FBI*.

THE DIRECTOR INSISTED THAT THE BUREAU'S SUCCESSES WERE THE RESULT OF TEAMWORK, NOT INDIVIDUAL HEROES . . .

. . . YET THE PUBLIC THIRSTED FOR HEROES, THE CLOSEST AT HAND BEING . . . THE DIRECTOR HIMSELF!

HOOVER'S WARTIME SPEECHES EMPHASIZED A STRONG AMERICAN FAMILY AS BULWARK OF MORALITY.

THE HOME, IN MANY WAYS, IS IMPERILED. WHEN THE HOME IS DESTROYED, EVERYTHING IN OUR CIVILIZATION CRASHES TO ITS DOOM.

HE INITIATED A THREE-POINT PROGRAM AS THE FOUNDATION OF HIS HOME-FRONT SECURITY EFFORT.

THE FIRST POINT BEING THE WORK OF LOCAL POLICE IN ROOTING OUT SUBVERSIVE ACTIVITY.

THE SECOND POINT WAS THE NETWORK OF INFORMANTS IN THE NATION'S DEFENSE PLANTS.

THE THIRD POINT WAS THE GRASS-ROOTS COUNTERESPIONAGE WORK OF THE AMERICAN LEGION AND OTHER PATRIOTIC ORGANIZATIONS.

THIS GAVE THE BUREAU JUSTIFICATION TO MONITOR THE ACTIVITIES OF SUCH GROUPS.

52

THE FBI SCORED ITS GREATEST WARTIME TRIUMPH WITH THE CAPTURE OF EIGHT NAZI SABOTEURS...

...FOUR OF WHOM CAME ASHORE ON JUNE 13, 1942, DEPOSITED BY A SUBMARINE OFF LONG ISLAND; THE OTHERS LANDED ON JUNE 17 IN FLORIDA.

SIX OF THE SABOTEURS MADE THEIR WAY TO NEW YORK CITY...

...BUT ALL EIGHT WERE ROUNDED UP BY AGENTS BEFORE DOING ANY DAMAGE.

HOOVER BASKED IN THE REFLECTED GLORY.

The New York Times

FBI CAPTURES 8 GERMAN AGENTS LANDED BY SUBS

YEARS LATER, IT WAS REVEALED THAT ONE OF THE GROUP'S LEADERS—DASCH—WAS A SYMPATHIZER OF THE U.S. WHO HAD SURRENDERED AND INFORMED UPON THE ENTIRE OPERATION.

THROUGHOUT THE WAR, HOOVER AND ROOSEVELT CONTINUED TO FIND EACH OTHER MUTUALLY USEFUL.

ALTHOUGH THE DIRECTOR DISAPPROVED OF THE CHIEF EXECUTIVE'S CONVIVIAL, HEAVY-DRINKING PERSONAL LIFE.

THE FIRST LADY DID NOT SHARE HER HUSBAND'S CAMARADERIE WITH THE DIRECTOR.

TO HER, THE FBI WAS ONE STEP AWAY FROM BECOMING AN AMERICAN GESTAPO.

TO HOOVER, MRS. ROOSEVELT WAS THE WORST SORT OF "SENTIMENTAL MOO-COW" . . .

. . . A BLEEDING HEART FOR THE ENEMIES OF AMERICAN SOCIETY.

ACCORDINGLY, HE HAD HER FOLLOWED ALONG EVERY MILE OF HER FAR-FLUNG TRAVELS . . .

. . . EVENTUALLY COMPILING A FAT DOSSIER OF WHERE SHE WENT, WHOM SHE MET, AND SO ON.

A PARTICULARLY DAMNING PIECE OF INFORMATION CONCERNED THE FIRST LADY AND HER FRIEND THE WRITER JOSEPH LASH.

THE ARMY'S INTELLIGENCE DIVISION HAD PLANTED A MICROPHONE IN HER CHICAGO HOTEL ROOM . . .

. . . AND THERE SUPPOSEDLY RECORDED HER AND LASH HAVING SEXUAL RELATIONS!

THE FACT THAT THE REPORT WAS TOTALLY UNFOUNDED DID NOT PREVENT ITS INCLUSION IN THE DIRECTOR'S "PERSONAL AND CONFIDENTIAL" FILE.

(IF ANYTHING, THE ARMY HAD RECORDED LASH HAVING RELATIONS WITH HIS OWN SECRET PARAMOUR— A RELATIONSHIP FACILITATED BY MRS. ROOSEVELT.)

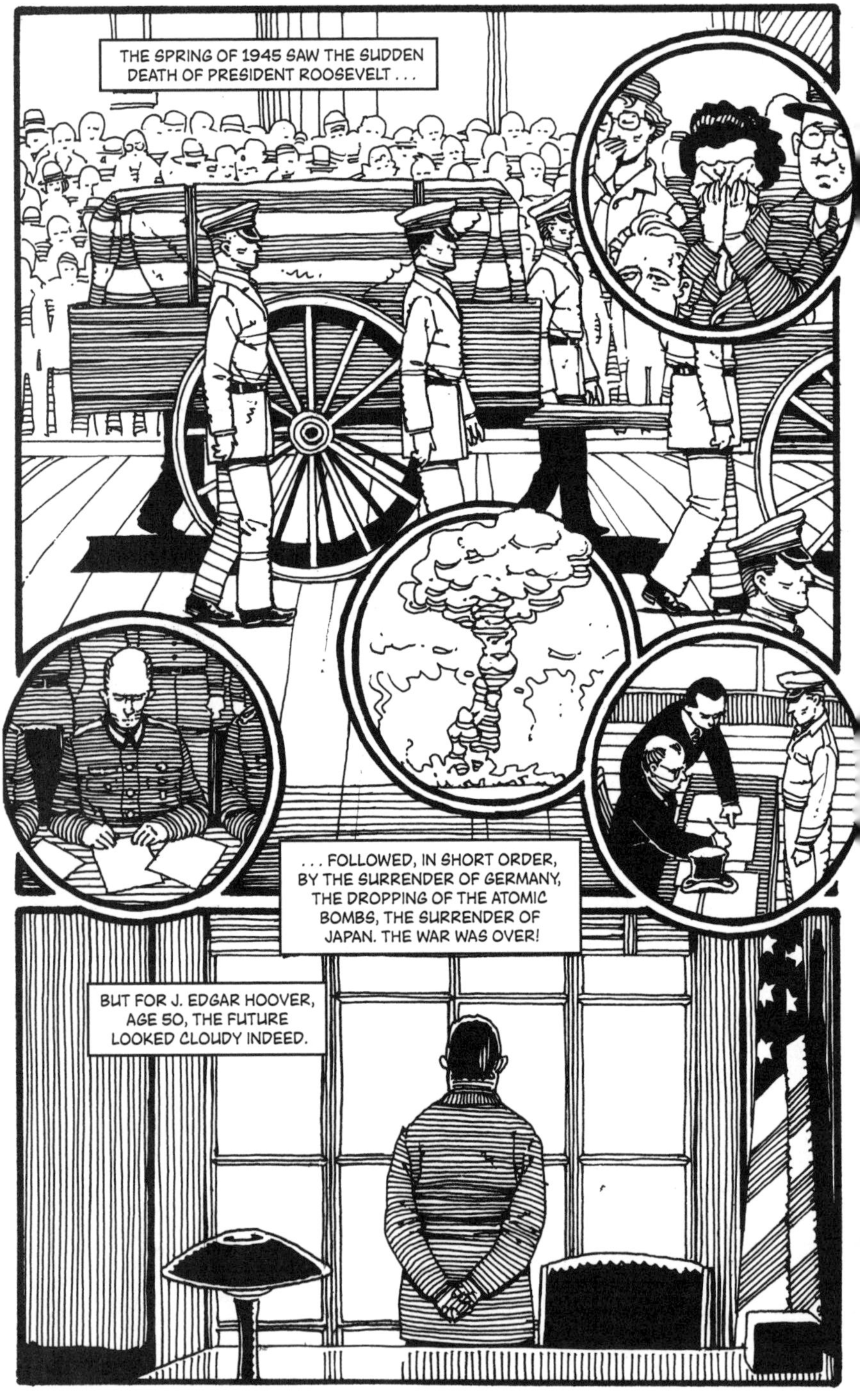
THE SPRING OF 1945 SAW THE SUDDEN DEATH OF PRESIDENT ROOSEVELT . . .
. . . FOLLOWED, IN SHORT ORDER, BY THE SURRENDER OF GERMANY, THE DROPPING OF THE ATOMIC BOMBS, THE SURRENDER OF JAPAN. THE WAR WAS OVER!
BUT FOR J. EDGAR HOOVER, AGE 50, THE FUTURE LOOKED CLOUDY INDEED.

PART VII
COLD WAR

THE NEW PRESIDENT, HARRY S. TRUMAN, HAD NO LOVE FOR THE FBI, WHICH HE CONSIDERED A THREAT TO CIVIL LIBERTIES.

YET, FOR THE SAKE OF CONTINUITY, HE AND HIS NEW ATTORNEY GENERAL, TOM CLARK, DECIDED TO KEEP HOOVER ON.

WITH EASTERN EUROPE FALLING TO SOVIET DOMINATION, A NEW RED SCARE SWEPT AMERICA.

COULD IT HAPPEN HERE?

HOOVER KNEW THAT IT COULD, AND, WITH THE END OF THE WAR, HE DESPERATELY DESIRED THAT HIS BUREAU TAKE OVER WORLDWIDE INTELLIGENCE OPERATIONS . . .

. . . AND WAS PROFOUNDLY DISAPPOINTED WHEN TRUMAN MADE FROM THE OLD OSS A NEW ORGANIZATION—THE CENTRAL INTELLIGENCE AGENCY.

HE IMMEDIATELY ORDERED A POLICY OF NONCOOPERATION BETWEEN THE FBI AND THIS UPSTART GROUP.

WITH LITTLE SUPPORT COMING FROM THE EXECUTIVE BRANCH, HOOVER SWITCHED HIS ALLEGIANCE TO THE NEWLY REPUBLICAN CONGRESS.

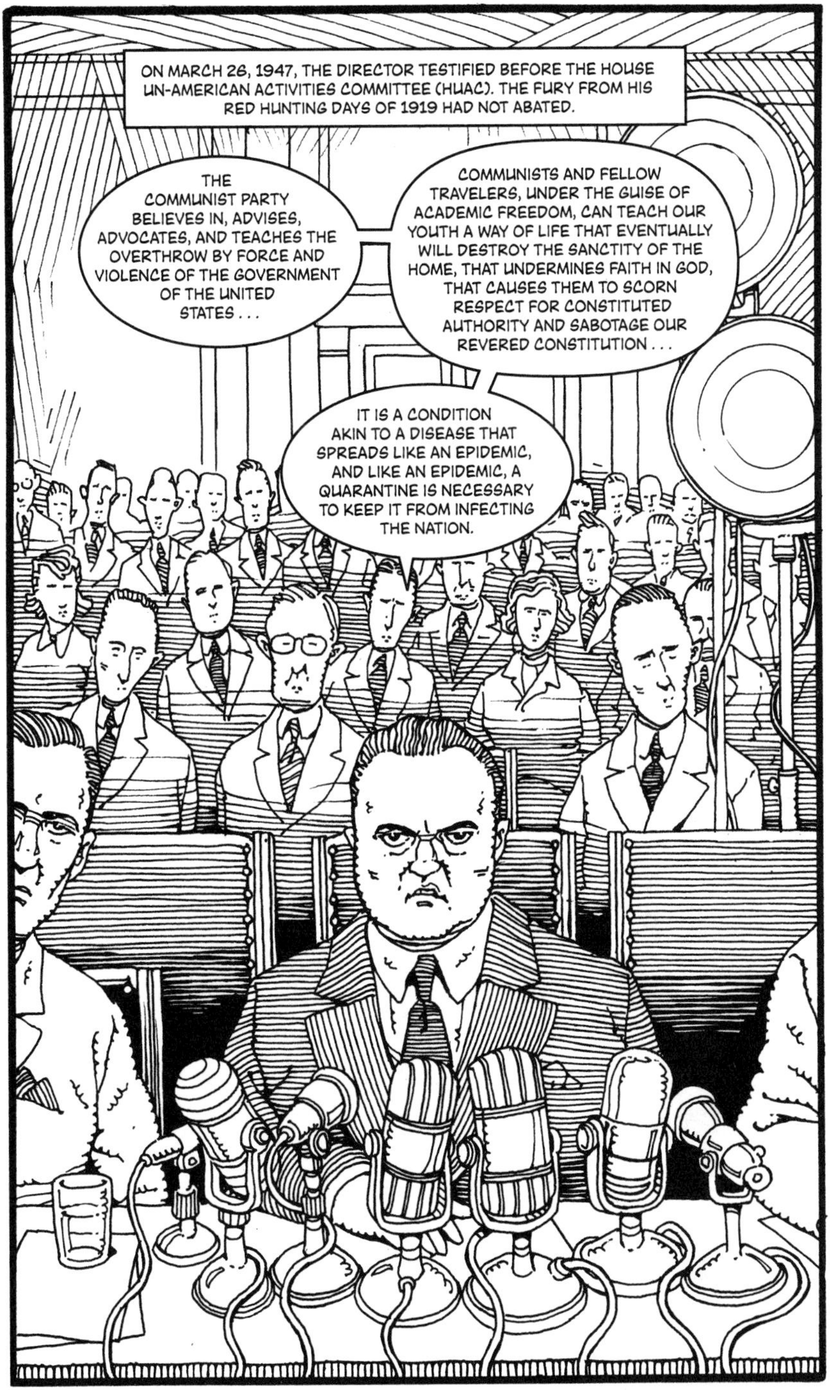
ON MARCH 26, 1947, THE DIRECTOR TESTIFIED BEFORE THE HOUSE UN-AMERICAN ACTIVITIES COMMITTEE (HUAC). THE FURY FROM HIS RED HUNTING DAYS OF 1919 HAD NOT ABATED.
THE COMMUNIST PARTY BELIEVES IN, ADVISES, ADVOCATES, AND TEACHES THE OVERTHROW BY FORCE AND VIOLENCE OF THE GOVERNMENT OF THE UNITED STATES . . .
COMMUNISTS AND FELLOW TRAVELERS, UNDER THE GUISE OF ACADEMIC FREEDOM, CAN TEACH OUR YOUTH A WAY OF LIFE THAT EVENTUALLY WILL DESTROY THE SANCTITY OF THE HOME, THAT UNDERMINES FAITH IN GOD, THAT CAUSES THEM TO SCORN RESPECT FOR CONSTITUTED AUTHORITY AND SABOTAGE OUR REVERED CONSTITUTION . . .
IT IS A CONDITION AKIN TO A DISEASE THAT SPREADS LIKE AN EPIDEMIC, AND LIKE AN EPIDEMIC, A QUARANTINE IS NECESSARY TO KEEP IT FROM INFECTING THE NATION.

LIKE MANY AMERICANS, HOOVER BELIEVED THAT WAR WITH THE SOVIET UNION WAS INEVITABLE...

...AND HE WAS DETERMINED NOT TO MISS ANY SIGNS POINTING TO A NEW PEARL HARBOR.

THE FEDERAL GOVERNMENT WAS TEEMING, HE WAS CERTAIN, WITH DANGEROUS "FELLOW TRAVELERS" FROM THE ROOSEVELT DAYS.

TRUMAN, HOWEVER, DISMISSED SUCH CONCERNS AS A "RED HERRING." TO HIM, HOOVER WAS SIMPLY JOCKEYING FOR POLITICAL POSITION.

THE WHITE HOUSE INSTITUTED A LOYALTY PROGRAM FOR GOVERNMENT WORKERS, BUT ONE IN WHICH THE FBI WOULD PLAY ONLY A MODEST ROLE.

I hereby swear

THIS INFURIATED THE DIRECTOR.

AS THE ELECTION OF 1948 APPROACHED, HOOVER WORKED SECRETLY FOR TRUMAN'S OPPONENT, GOVERNOR THOMAS E. DEWEY OF NEW YORK...

FOR
RESIDE

...WITH THE HOPE, SOME SAID, OF BECOMING ATTORNEY GENERAL.

IN THE SUMMER OF 1948, DURING THE HEIGHT OF THE PRESIDENTIAL CAMPAIGN, HUAC HELD HEARINGS INTO THE ACCUSATIONS OF WHITTAKER CHAMBERS, A REFORMED COMMUNIST AND CLOSE ASSOCIATE OF J. EDGAR HOOVER.

CHAMBERS ACCUSED SEVERAL FEDERAL OFFICIALS OF HAVING PASSED SECRETS TO THE SOVIETS—CHIEF AMONG THEM ALGER HISS, A FORMER STATE DEPARTMENT DIPLOMAT.

HISS, HOWEVER, CLAIMED NEVER TO HAVE BEEN A COMMUNIST, AND NEVER TO HAVE MET CHAMBERS.

GIVING THE ACCUSED AN ESPECIALLY VIGOROUS CROSS-EXAMINATION WAS A YOUNG CONGRESSMAN FROM CALIFORNIA— RICHARD M. NIXON.

DESPITE THE WIRETAPPING OF HISS'S HOME, HOOVER FOUND NO INFORMATION THAT THE COMMITTEE COULD USE AGAINST HIM.

THE HEARINGS ENDED AMBIGUOUSLY (ALTHOUGH HISS WOULD LATER BE CONVICTED OF PERJURY), AND TRUMAN SQUEAKED THROUGH TO VICTORY IN NOVEMBER.

Chicago

DEWEY DE

61

HOOVER'S GREATEST TOOL DURING THIS PERIOD WAS THE SMITH ACT OF 1940, WHICH PROVIDED FOR THE ARREST OF ANYBODY ADVOCATING THE OVERTHROW OF THE U.S. GOVERNMENT BY FORCE OR VIOLENCE . . .

. . . OR A MEMBER OF ANY GROUP THAT ADVOCATED THE SAME.

THE ACT WAS USED TO INDICT AND CONVICT 12 MEMBERS OF THE COMMUNIST PARTY'S NATIONAL BOARD IN 1949.

BUT THIS WAS NOT ENOUGH FOR THE DIRECTOR.

OVER THE NEXT SEVERAL MONTHS, THE FBI ROUNDED UP 126 PARTY LEADERS, OUT OF WHICH 93 WERE CONVICTED . . .

. . . DEMORALIZING AND MARGINALIZING THE COMMUNIST CAUSE IN THE U.S. AS NEVER BEFORE.

NEVERTHELESS, AT THIS TIME AN OBSCURE SENATOR FROM WISCONSIN WAS TRYING TO MAKE A NAME FOR HIMSELF. JOSEPH R. McCARTHY MADE THE SURPRISING CLAIM THAT THE U.S. STATE DEPARTMENT WAS FULL OF ACTIVE COMMUNISTS.

I HAVE HERE IN MY HAND A LIST OF 205—A LIST OF NAMES THAT WERE KNOWN TO THE SECRETARY OF STATE AND WHO, NEVERTHELESS, ARE STILL WORKING AND SHAPING THE POLICY OF THE STATE DEPARTMENT.

IN THE FALL OF 1948, HUAC TRAVELED TO THE WEST COAST TO CONDUCT HEARINGS ON COMMUNIST INFLUENCE IN THE FILM INDUSTRY.

HOOVER SUPPLIED THE COMMITTEE WITH INFORMATION GATHERED FROM EXTENSIVE SURVEILLANCE OF ACTORS, WRITERS, DIRECTORS, AND SO ON.

THE POLITICALLY MINDED ACTOR RONALD REAGAN, AMONG OTHERS, TESTIFIED AS A "FRIENDLY" WITNESS.

THE HEARINGS RESULTED IN AN INDUSTRY-WIDE BLACKLIST AND THE DESTRUCTION OF HUNDREDS OF CAREERS.

CHARLES CHAPLIN, AMONG OTHERS, LEFT THE COUNTRY, NEVER TO RETURN.

IN THE SAME WAY, HOOVER ATTEMPTED TO INFLUENCE HIRING AT MAJOR UNIVERSITIES AND PUBLISHING HOUSES.

THOSE ACADEMICS WHO HAD UTTERED EVEN THE SLIGHTEST CRITICISM OF THE FBI AND ITS METHODS WERE DEEMED DANGEROUS AND UNSUITABLE.

IN 1950, THE MOST SENSATIONAL SPY CASE OF THE ERA BROKE WITH THE ARREST OF JULIUS AND ETHEL ROSENBERG...

...A NEW YORK LEFTIST COUPLE ACCUSED OF PASSING ATOMIC SECRETS TO THE SOVIETS.

BY THIS TIME, THE COLD WAR HAD TURNED HOT, AND U.S. SOLDIERS WERE FIGHTING THE COMMUNISTS IN KOREA...

CHINA

38° PARALLEL

SEOUL

JAPAN

...AND EVERY SETBACK WAS SEEN AS THE PRODUCT OF TRAITOROUS ACTIVITY AT HOME.

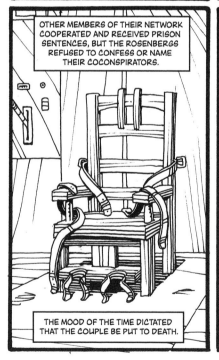

OTHER MEMBERS OF THEIR NETWORK COOPERATED AND RECEIVED PRISON SENTENCES, BUT THE ROSENBERGS REFUSED TO CONFESS OR NAME THEIR COCONSPIRATORS.

THE MOOD OF THE TIME DICTATED THAT THE COUPLE BE PUT TO DEATH.

AT THE TRIAL'S CONCLUSION, JUDGE IRVING R. KAUFMAN SINGLED OUT ONE PERSON FOR PRAISE.

GREAT TRIBUTE IS DUE TO THE FBI AND MR. HOOVER FOR THE SPLENDID JOB THEY HAVE DONE IN THIS CASE.

64

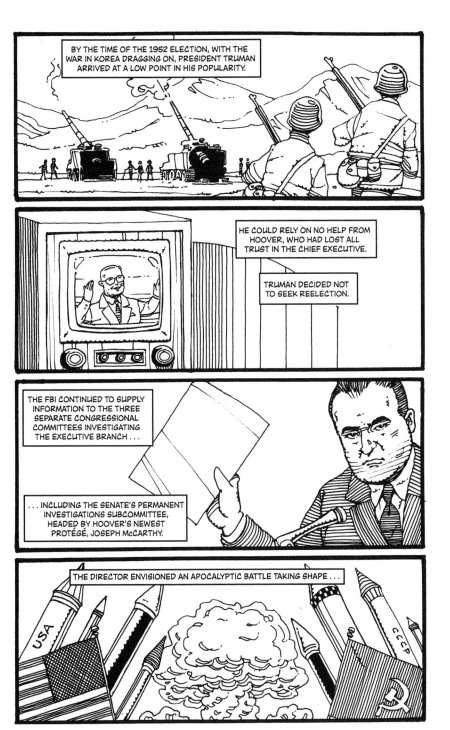

BY THE TIME OF THE 1952 ELECTION, WITH THE WAR IN KOREA DRAGGING ON, PRESIDENT TRUMAN ARRIVED AT A LOW POINT IN HIS POPULARITY.

HE COULD RELY ON NO HELP FROM HOOVER, WHO HAD LOST ALL TRUST IN THE CHIEF EXECUTIVE.

TRUMAN DECIDED NOT TO SEEK REELECTION.

THE FBI CONTINUED TO SUPPLY INFORMATION TO THE THREE SEPARATE CONGRESSIONAL COMMITTEES INVESTIGATING THE EXECUTIVE BRANCH . . .

. . . INCLUDING THE SENATE'S PERMANENT INVESTIGATIONS SUBCOMMITTEE, HEADED BY HOOVER'S NEWEST PROTÉGÉ, JOSEPH MCCARTHY.

THE DIRECTOR ENVISIONED AN APOCALYPTIC BATTLE TAKING SHAPE . . .

USA

CCCP

. . . THE FINAL WAR BETWEEN THE FORCES OF GOD-FEARING AMERICANISM AND GODLESS SECULARISM.

COMMUNISM IS SECULARISM ON THE MARCH. IT IS A MORAL FOE OF CHRISTIANITY. EITHER IT WILL SURVIVE OR CHRISTIANITY WILL TRIUMPH, BECAUSE IN THIS LAND OF OURS THE TWO CANNOT LIVE SIDE BY SIDE.

IN HOOVER'S EYES, A HERO NOW AROSE. GENERAL DWIGHT EISENHOWER WAS ELECTED PRESIDENT, AND WITH HIM, AS VICE PRESIDENT, THE FAMOUS RED HUNTER RICHARD NIXON.

PART VIII

PINNACLE OF POWER

HOOVER WAS AGAIN WELCOME AT THE WHITE HOUSE. THE NEW PRESIDENT PLACED ABSOLUTE TRUST IN THE FBI DIRECTOR, AS DID THE NEW ATTORNEY GENERAL, HERBERT BROWNELL.

WELCOME

THE FBI WAS BACK IN CHARGE OF LOYALTY INVESTIGATIONS OF GOVERNMENT WORKERS.

HOOVER CONTINUED SUPPLYING RAW INFORMATION TO JOSEPH McCARTHY, HIS SUBCOMMITTEE, AND ITS NEW CHIEF COUNSEL, ROY COHN.

HOWEVER, WHEN McCARTHY'S CRUSADE CAME INTO CONFLICT WITH THE EISENHOWER ADMINISTRATION, HOOVER'S ALLEGIANCE REMAINED WITH THE PRESIDENT.

WHEN THE SUBCOMMITTEE BEGAN TO INVESTIGATE SUBVERSION WITHIN THE U.S. ARMY, THE SENATOR GREW EVER MORE RECKLESS IN HIS ACCUSATIONS.

THE ARMY-McCARTHY HEARINGS OF MARCH 1954 SAW THE BEGINNING OF THE SENATOR'S DECLINE. THE ARMY'S COUNSEL, JOSEPH WELCH, DEALT THE FINAL BLOW.

HAVE YOU NO SENSE OF DECENCY, SIR?

HOOVER COULD DO NOTHING BUT WATCH HIS FRIEND SELF-DESTRUCT.

BY NOW, THE DIRECTOR HAD, IN HIS PERSONAL LIFE, ATTAINED A LEVEL OF SECURITY AND ORDER THAT HE WISHED FOR THE AMERICAN PEOPLE.

HE WOULD LATER SAY THAT THE EISENHOWER YEARS WERE THE "BEST AND HAPPIEST" OF HIS LIFE.

THE WALLS OF HIS HOME WERE COVERED WITH PHOTOS OF THE PEOPLE HE HAD MET, THE PLACES HE HAD VISITED . . .

. . . WHILE DOWNSTAIRS, HE MAINTAINED A MASCULINE "DEN," COMPLETE WITH BAR, POOL TABLE, AND PINUPS . . .

. . . WHERE HE WOULD ENTERTAIN AN UNCHANGING GROUP OF MALE FRIENDS.

FOR PETS, HE KEPT A SUCCESSION OF CAIRN TERRIERS, ONE OF THEM ALWAYS NAMED G-BOY.

CLYDE TOLSON REMAINED HIS CLOSEST CONFIDANT AND COMPANION, BOTH PUBLIC AND PRIVATE . . .

. . . AS RUMORS CONTINUED TO SWIRL ABOUT THEIR SUPPOSED SEXUAL RELATIONSHIP.

THE DIRECTOR DID NOT HESITATE TO SEND AGENTS TO TRACK DOWN THE SOURCE FOR ANY SUCH RUMOR.

THOSE INTERVIEWED WOULD BECOME PART OF A NEW FILE.

ANOTHER SCHOOL OF THOUGHT HELD THAT THE RUMORS WERE WRONG— THAT HOOVER, AS AN AUTHORITARIAN PERSONALITY, WAS FEARFUL OF HIS OWN SEXUALITY AND WOULD ACTIVELY SUPPRESS SUCH DESIRES.

FROM THESE YEARS CAME AN ACCOUNT OF THE DIRECTOR IN DRESS AND WIG—AND REQUESTING TO BE CALLED MARY—AT A PRIVATE PARTY IN THE PLAZA HOTEL IN NEW YORK.

BUT THE STORY, TOLD BY A SINGLE UNRELIABLE WITNESS, SEEMED, TO MANY, OUT OF CHARACTER FOR THE OBSESSIVELY SECRETIVE HOOVER.

THE VACATION TRIPS THAT HOOVER AND TOLSON TOOK EACH YEAR WERE USUALLY WRITTEN OFF AS "BUREAU BUSINESS" AND PAID FOR BY THE PUBLIC.

CHRISTMAS AND NEW YEAR AT THE GULFSTREAM HOTEL IN MIAMI . . .

SUMMERS IN LA JOLLA, CALIFORNIA . . .

. . . WHERE THEY OCCUPIED A SPECIAL BUNGALOW AT THE DEL CHARRO HOTEL, OWNED BY HOOVER'S FRIEND THE TEXAS OIL MILLIONAIRE CLINT MURCHISON.

THEY WERE DAILY ATTENDEES AT THE DEL MAR RACETRACK NORTH OF LA JOLLA, ALSO OWNED BY THE OILMAN.

DEL MAR

LA JOLLA

SAN DIEGO

TIJUANA

MEXIC

MURCHISON AND HIS FELLOW MILLIONAIRE SID RICHARDSON SHARED HOOVER'S POLITICAL LEANINGS.

MURCHISON

RICHARDSON

THEY PLIED THE DIRECTOR WITH GIFTS AND INVESTMENT TIPS THAT EVENTUALLY MADE HIM AND TOLSON QUITE WEALTHY.

71

HOOVER HAD BY THIS TIME MADE OF THE FBI AN ABSOLUTE DICTATORSHIP.

OFFICE of the DIRECTOR

HE WOULD BROOK NO CRITICISM OR INSUBORDINATION FROM HIS AGENTS, WHO WORKED IN AN ATMOSPHERE OF FEAR AND INSECURITY.

AGENTS DREADED ANY MEETING WITH THE DIRECTOR...

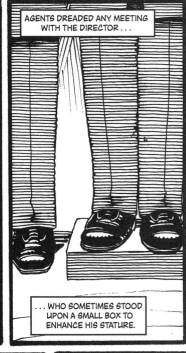

...WHO SOMETIMES STOOD UPON A SMALL BOX TO ENHANCE HIS STATURE.

THOSE NOT FITTING HIS EXACTING PHYSICAL STANDARDS—

WHO WERE OVERWEIGHT, HAD BAD SKIN, THINNING HAIR, OR PROTRUDING EARS—WERE DEEMED UNSUITABLE TO THE BUREAU'S IMAGE.

HOOVER EVEN RESERVED FOR HIMSELF THE RIGHT TO APPROVE AN AGENT'S MARRIAGE.

ARBITRARY AND PUNITIVE TRANSFERS BECAME KNOWN AMONG AGENTS AS THE "BUREAU BICYCLE."

AN AGENT COULD ADVANCE ONLY BY REINFORCING THE DIRECTOR'S PREJUDICES.

THUS, LIKE ALL DICTATORS, HE LIVED IN A WORLD FREE OF CONTRADICTION AND WITHOUT ACCESS TO INDEPENDENT JUDGMENT.

72

1956 SAW THE PUBLICATION OF THE FIRST FULL-SCALE AUTHORIZED HISTORY OF THE BUREAU: *THE FBI STORY* BY DON WHITEHEAD . . .

. . . WRITTEN IN COOPERATION WITH LOUIS NICHOLS AND THE CRIME RECORDS DIVISION.

THREE YEARS LATER, IT WAS ADAPTED INTO A MOVIE . . .

. . . STARRING JAMES STEWART AS A HEROIC AGENT AND VERA MILES AS HIS LOYAL WIFE.

IN 1958, HOOVER'S OWN BOOK, *MASTERS OF DECEIT*, WAS PUBLISHED.

MASTERS OF DECEIT

The Story of Communism In America and How to Fight it.

J. EDGAR HOOVER

THIS EXPOSÉ OF THE EVILS OF COMMUNISM BECAME A NATIONAL BESTSELLER.

HOOVER, IN REALITY, HAD NO HAND IN WRITING THE BOOK, WHICH WAS THE PRODUCT OF SEVERAL BUREAU EMPLOYEES, WORKING ON PUBLIC TIME.

THE ROYALTIES, THOUGH NOMINALLY DEDICATED TO THE BUREAU'S RECREATION FUND, WERE LARGELY POCKETED BY THE DIRECTOR, TOLSON, AND NICHOLS.

AS THE 1950S PROGRESSED, THE COLD WAR SIMMERED AND U.S.-SOVIET RELATIONS REACHED AN ALL-TIME LOW.

WE WILL BURY YOU!

CHAIRMAN NIKITA KHRUSHCHEV STRUCK FEAR INTO AMERICAN HEARTS.

THE AMERICAN COMMUNIST PARTY, HOWEVER, WAS WANING IN INFLUENCE, REDUCED TO PERHAPS 4,000 MEMBERS NATIONALLY.

YET TO HOOVER, IT REMAINED A GRAVE THREAT, WITH TENTACLES REACHING INTO ALL ASPECTS OF NATIONAL LIFE.

IN 1956, HE INITIATED A SECRET CAMPAIGN DESIGNED TO DESTROY THE PARTY ONCE AND FOR ALL.

COINTELPRO

THE COUNTERINTELLIGENCE PROGRAMS, OR COINTELPRO.

GOING BEYOND MERE TRACKING AND SURVEILLANCE, COINTELPRO WAS NOT DESIGNED TO BRING WRONGDOERS TO JUSTICE . . .

ORKERS of the

. . . BUT TO DISRUPT, HARASS, AND UNDERMINE ACTIVITIES THAT WERE PERFECTLY LEGAL.

THE VARIOUS SUBTERFUGES OF THE PROGRAM INCLUDED THE FOLLOWING:

PLANTING FALSE "STORIES" IN THE MEDIA.

ANONYMOUS LETTERS AND TELEPHONE CALLS . . .

. . . THAT WOULD ACCUSE AN INDIVIDUAL OF ADULTERY OR SEXUAL DEVIANCE.

PLANTING "EVIDENCE" THAT A PARTY MEMBER WAS, IN FACT, AN FBI INFORMANT.

(THIS WAS CALLED A "SNITCH JACKET.")

SENDING AGENTS TO AN INDIVIDUAL'S PLACE OF EMPLOYMENT . . .

. . . A SIMPLE ACT THAT WOULD OFTEN GUARANTEE THAT PERSON'S DISMISSAL.

IT WAS SAID THAT BY THE END OF THE DECADE . . .

. . . THE COMMUNIST PARTY USA WAS MADE UP OF MORE FBI INFORMANTS THAN SINCERE BELIEVERS.

THE PROBLEM OF ORGANIZED CRIME MADE THE HEADLINES IN NOVEMBER 1957 . . .

. . . WHEN A LARGE CONFERENCE OF CRIMINAL SYNDICATE LEADERS WAS OBSERVED AT AN ESTATE IN APALACHIN, N.Y.

MANY WONDERED WHY THE FBI HAD MADE THE NATIONAL SYNDICATES SUCH A LOW PRIORITY OVER THE YEARS. THE DIRECTOR OFTEN SAID . . .

ORGANIZED CRIME DOES NOT EXIST.

THE DIRECTOR SIMPLY DID NOT WANT TO GET HIS AGENTS INVOLVED. SEVERAL REASONS FOR THIS WERE GIVEN: HE DID NOT WANT HIS MEN SUBJECT TO THE TEMPTATION OF LARGE BRIBES AND PAYOFFS; HE DID NOT FEEL THAT THE FBI HAD JURISDICTION—AFTER ALL, CRIME WAS ESSENTIALLY A LOCAL PROBLEM (ALTHOUGH IN THE PAST HE HAD ALWAYS FOUND WAYS TO MAKE A LOCAL CRIME FEDERAL IF HE SO DESIRED) . . .

. . . SOME SPECULATED THAT HE RESISTED THE COORDINATION WITH OTHER AGENCIES THAT SUCH AN OPERATION WOULD INVOLVE . . .

. . . OR THAT, CASES AGAINST MOBSTERS BEING NOTORIOUSLY HARD TO PROVE, HE FEARED BLEMISHING THE BUREAU'S HIGH CONVICTION RATE.

ANOTHER REASON MAY HAVE BEEN HOOVER'S CLOSE ASSOCIATION WITH CERTAIN MAFIA FIGURES, NURTURED OVER THE YEARS AT THE RACES OR THE STORK CLUB.

THE NEW YORK BOSS FRANK COSTELLO BRAGGED THAT HE SOMETIMES MADE SURE HOOVER WON AT THE TRACK.

MOB MONEYMAN MEYER LANSKY ONCE BOASTED:

HOOVER'S NOT A PROBLEM.

DID THE MOB HAVE SOMETHING ON THE DIRECTOR—PERHAPS COMPROMISING PHOTOGRAPHS?

NO EVIDENCE FOR THIS HAS EVER BEEN DISCOVERED.

IN RESPONSE TO PRESSURE FROM THE NEW ATTORNEY GENERAL, WILLIAM ROGERS, HOOVER GRUDGINGLY ESTABLISHED THE "TOP HOODLUM PROGRAM," INDEPENDENT OF ANY OTHER GOVERNMENT AGENCY.

BUT THE EFFORT WAS HALFHEARTED AT BEST. BY DECADE'S END, THE FBI'S NEW YORK OFFICE HAD 400 AGENTS INVESTIGATING COMMUNISTS, AND JUST FOUR LOOKING AT ORGANIZED CRIME.

IT WAS NOW 1960, AND J. EDGAR HOOVER, AT AGE 65, WAS ABOUT TO SEE HIS WORLD CHANGE DRAMATICALLY.

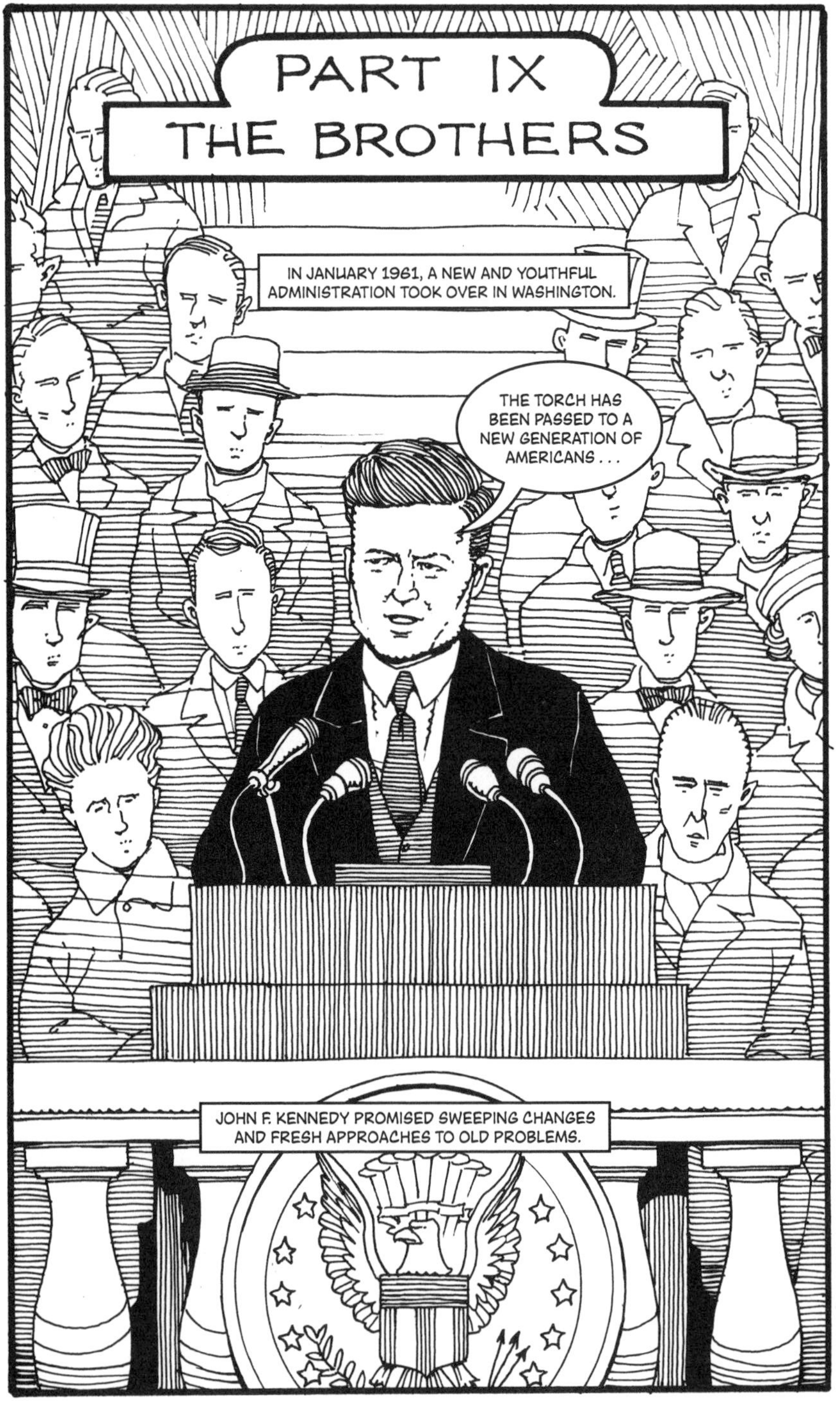
PART IX
THE BROTHERS
IN JANUARY 1961, A NEW AND YOUTHFUL ADMINISTRATION TOOK OVER IN WASHINGTON.
THE TORCH HAS BEEN PASSED TO A NEW GENERATION OF AMERICANS . . .
JOHN F. KENNEDY PROMISED SWEEPING CHANGES AND FRESH APPROACHES TO OLD PROBLEMS.

JOSEPH KENNEDY, THE NEW PRESIDENT'S FATHER, HAD BEEN A FRIEND OF HOOVER'S SINCE THE DAYS OF PROHIBITION, DURING WHICH TIME THE FINANCIER WAS AN ACTIVE BOOTLEGGER.

BUT THE ELDER KENNEDY'S 1961 STROKE LARGELY ENDED HIS INFLUENCE.

THE FBI HAD KEPT A FILE ON JACK KENNEDY SINCE 1941 . . .

. . . WHEN THE YOUNG MAN CARRIED ON A LOVE AFFAIR WITH INGA ARVAD, A DANISH BEAUTY QUEEN THOUGHT TO BE A NAZI SPY.

FROM THE BEGINNING, HOOVER'S RELATIONS WITH ROBERT KENNEDY, THE NEW ATTORNEY GENERAL, WERE PRICKLY.

THE YOUNGER MAN RAN HIS OFFICE WITH AN INFORMALITY THAT WAS INTOLERABLE TO THE FBI DIRECTOR.

IT INFURIATED HOOVER THAT THE ATTORNEY GENERAL WOULD SIMPLY WALK INTO HIS OFFICE WITHOUT AN APPOINTMENT . . .

. . . OR USE A BUZZER TO SUMMON THE OLDER MAN, AS IF HE WERE AN INSIGNIFICANT UNDERLING.

KENNEDY PRESSURED HOOVER TO HIRE MORE BLACK AGENTS. AT THE TIME, THE BUREAU HAD JUST FIVE BLACK EMPLOYEES, ALL OF THEM SERVANTS OF THE DIRECTOR!

THESE INCLUDED SAM NOISETTE, WHO SERVED AS DOORKEEPER IN HOOVER'S OFFICE, AND JAMES CRAWFORD, HIS CHAUFFEUR.

AS THE PRODUCT OF A SEGREGATED SOUTHERN CITY, HOOVER'S RACIAL ATTITUDES WERE LITTLE DIFFERENT FROM MOST OF HIS GENERATION.

HE SAW BLACK PEOPLE LARGELY AS CHILDREN IN NEED OF GUIDANCE AND DISCIPLINE.

HOOVER MADE SURE THAT BOTH KENNEDYS WERE AWARE OF HIS CONSTANTLY UPDATED FILES.

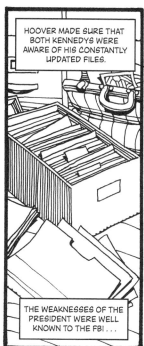

THE WEAKNESSES OF THE PRESIDENT WERE WELL KNOWN TO THE FBI...

HIS SEXUAL DALLIANCES WITH MARILYN MONROE, ANGIE DICKINSON, AND OTHER ACTRESSES...

...AND WITH JUDITH CAMPBELL, MISTRESS OF THE CHICAGO MOB BOSS SAM GIANCANA.

HOOVER WARNED THE PRESIDENT OF THE DANGERS OF THESE ATTACHMENTS AND OTHERS, SUCH AS HIS FRIENDSHIP WITH FRANK SINATRA...

...WHOSE CONNECTIONS WITH MOB FIGURES WERE ALSO KNOWN TO THE BUREAU.

THE FAILED 1961 INVASION OF CUBA AT THE BAY OF PIGS, BY CIA-BACKED EXILES INTENT UPON THE OVERTHROW OF FIDEL CASTRO, WAS A MAJOR EMBARRASSMENT TO THE FLEDGLING ADMINISTRATION.

CASTRO WAS A THORN IN THE SIDE OF THE U.S. GOVERNMENT...

...AND A CIA PLAN TO ASSASSINATE HIM HAD BEEN ONGOING SINCE THE EISENHOWER YEARS.

26 Julio

RENEWED EFFORTS INVOLVED THE EXPERTISE OF SAM GIANCANA AND HIS CHICAGO ASSOCIATE JOHNNY ROSELLI.

THE MAFIA HAD ITS OWN REASONS FOR ELIMINATING THE DICTATOR: HIS REVOLUTION HAD PUT AN END TO THEIR HIGHLY PROFITABLE CUBAN OPERATIONS.

BOTH ENTERPRISES ONLY REINFORCED HOOVER'S IRRITATION WITH THE OVERREACHING AND INCOMPETENCE OF THE CIA.

THE BURGEONING CIVIL RIGHTS MOVEMENT WAS SUPPORTED BY THE KENNEDY ADMINISTRATION . . .

STAND UP FOR CIVIL RIGHTS

UNITE FOR HUMAN DIGNIT

STICE OR ALL RICANS NOW!

. . . MUCH TO THE DISPLEASURE OF HOOVER, WHO SAW MALIGN INFLUENCE BEHIND ANY TALK OF "LIBERATION."

JUSTICE

HE REMEMBERED THE COMMUNIST TRACTS FROM HIS EARLY DAYS AT THE JUSTICE DEPARTMENT, WHICH STRESSED THE RECRUITMENT OF BLACK PEOPLE AS KEY TO REVOLUTION IN AMERICA.

WORLD WIDE

REVOLT!

UNITE

WORLD REVOLUTION

HANDBOOK

NEVERTHELESS, IN 1961 THE KENNEDYS SENT FEDERAL MARSHALS TO ALABAMA, TO PROTECT THE "FREEDOM RIDERS" . . .

. . . IN THEIR EFFORT TO DESEGREGATE INTERSTATE BUSES AND DEPOTS IN THE SOUTH.

LIKEWISE WHEN JAMES MEREDITH ATTEMPTED TO ENROLL AT THE UNIVERSITY OF MISSISSIPPI . . .

. . . AND WHEN GOVERNOR GEORGE WALLACE ATTEMPTED TO PREVENT BLACKS FROM ENTERING THE UNIVERSITY OF ALABAMA.

IN SEPTEMBER 1963, FOUR GIRLS DIED IN THE BOMBING OF A BLACK CHURCH IN BIRMINGHAM.

THE DIRECTOR RESISTED ALL PRESSURE BY THE ATTORNEY GENERAL TO INVOLVE THE FBI MORE DIRECTLY IN THIS EFFORT.

TO HIM, THE BUREAU WAS AN INVESTIGATIVE AGENCY ONLY, NOT A POLICE FORCE.

ON AUGUST 28, 1963, THE CIVIL RIGHTS MOVEMENT CULMINATED IN THE HUGE MARCH ON WASHINGTON.

I HAVE A DREAM . . .

THE WORDS OF THE REVEREND MARTIN LUTHER KING, JR., GALVANIZED THE NATION.

THE ACTIVITIES OF REVEREND KING HAD BEEN UNDER FBI SURVEILLANCE SINCE 1958 . . .

EQUAL RIGHTS NOW

. . . WHEN HE WAS THOUGHT TO HAVE TWO COMMUNISTS AS ADVISERS.

HOOVER'S PERSONAL ENMITY TOWARD KING HAD ITS ORIGINS IN AN OFFHAND COMMENT BY THE CIVIL-RIGHTS LEADER:

ONE OF THE GREAT PROBLEMS WE FACE WITH THE FBI IN THE SOUTH IS THAT THE AGENTS ARE WHITE SOUTHERNERS WHO HAVE BEEN INFLUENCED BY THE MORES OF THE COMMUNITY.

THESE WORDS, TO HOOVER, MADE THE REVEREND, EVER AFTER, A LIAR AND A FRAUD— SINCE, AT THE TIME, THE BUREAU ACTUALLY EMPLOYED MORE NORTHERN AGENTS IN ITS SOUTHERN FIELD OFFICES.

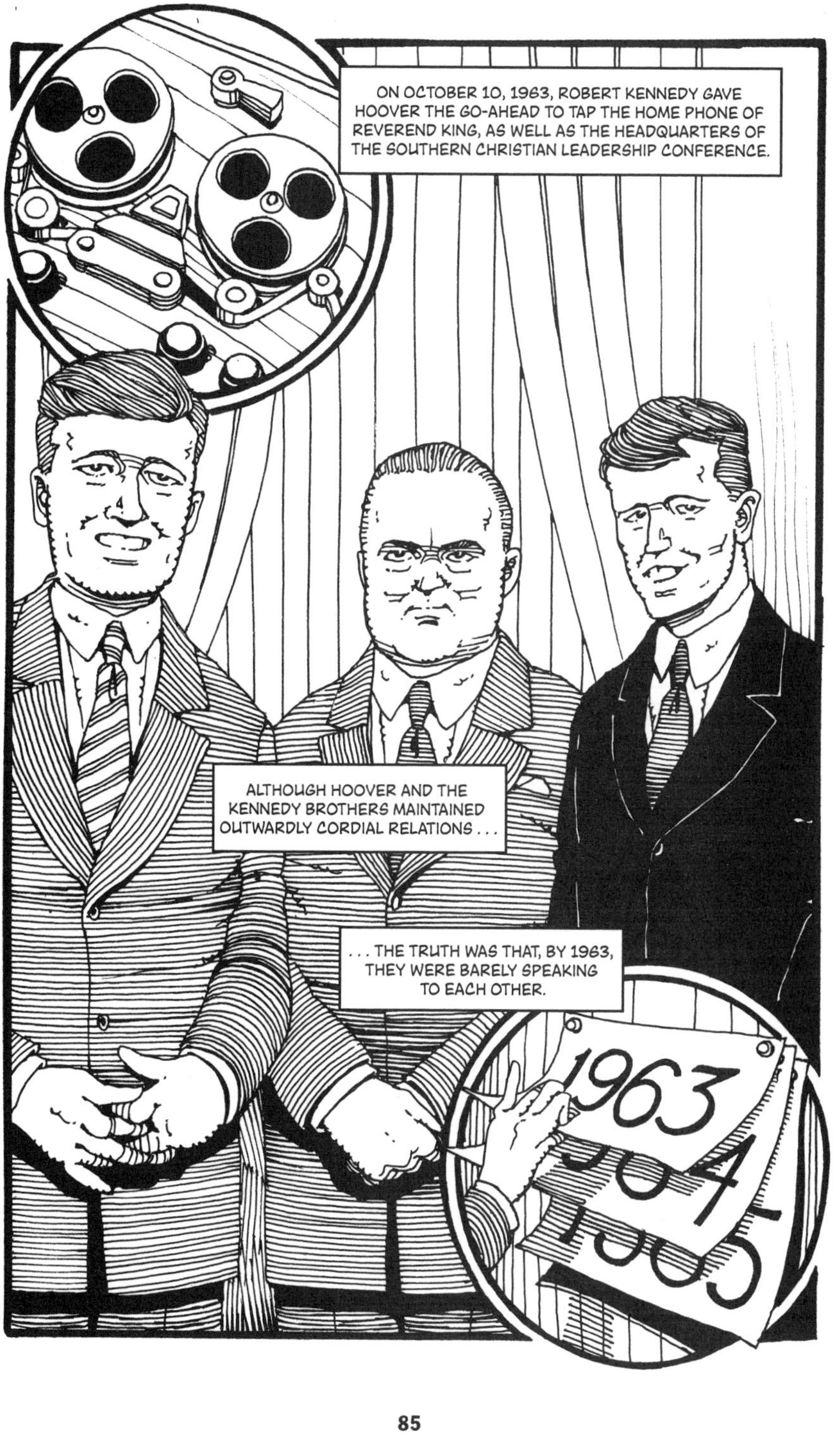
ON OCTOBER 10, 1963, ROBERT KENNEDY GAVE HOOVER THE GO-AHEAD TO TAP THE HOME PHONE OF REVEREND KING, AS WELL AS THE HEADQUARTERS OF THE SOUTHERN CHRISTIAN LEADERSHIP CONFERENCE.
ALTHOUGH HOOVER AND THE KENNEDY BROTHERS MAINTAINED OUTWARDLY CORDIAL RELATIONS . . .
. . . THE TRUTH WAS THAT, BY 1963, THEY WERE BARELY SPEAKING TO EACH OTHER.
1963

JOHN F. KENNEDY WAS SHOT AND KILLED IN DALLAS, TEXAS, ON NOVEMBER 22, 1963.

IT FELL TO HOOVER TO INFORM ROBERT KENNEDY OF THE TRAGEDY.

I HAVE NEWS FOR YOU... THE PRESIDENT'S BEEN SHOT.

KENNEDY WAS STRUCK BY HOOVER'S COLD, MATTER-OF-FACT TONE: "HE WAS NOT A VERY WARM OR SYMPATHETIC FIGURE."

THE NEW PRESIDENT, LYNDON JOHNSON, PROMISED TO CARRY ON THE KENNEDY PROGRAMS...

...THE DIFFERENCE BEING THAT JOHNSON LIKED AND RESPECTED THE FBI DIRECTOR.

THE TWO HAD, IN FACT, BEEN GOOD FRIENDS SINCE 1945, WHEN THEY LIVED IN THE SAME ROCK CREEK PARK NEIGHBORHOOD. HOOVER SOMETIMES BABYSAT THE JOHNSONS' TWO DAUGHTERS.

IN ADDITION, THEY SHARED AN ABIDING DISLIKE OF ROBERT KENNEDY.

WHEN THE WARREN COMMISSION GOT UNDER WAY TO INVESTIGATE THE KENNEDY ASSASSINATION, THE FBI WAS ITS MAJOR SOURCE OF INFORMATION.

THE DIRECTOR DISCOURAGED INPUT FROM ANY OTHER AGENCY.

WHILE THE BUREAU SUPPORTED THE CONCLUSION THAT LEE HARVEY OSWALD WAS THE LONE ASSASSIN...

...IT WAS FAULTED FOR ITS FAILURE TO TRACK THIS KNOWN COMMUNIST IN THE WEEKS BEFORE THE CRIME.

IN 1964, LYNDON JOHNSON WAS ELECTED TO A FULL TERM AND J. EDGAR HOOVER CELEBRATED 40 YEARS AS HEAD OF THE FBI.

F O R

L I F E !

THAT SUMMER, THE RACIAL STRUGGLE IN THE SOUTH TURNED DEADLIER WITH THE MURDERS OF THREE YOUNG CIVIL-RIGHTS WORKERS IN MISSISSIPPI—ANDREW GOODMAN, JAMES CHANEY, AND MICHAEL SCHWERNER.

TO SHOW HIS CONFIDENCE IN THE DIRECTOR, THE PRESIDENT WAIVED THE MANDATORY-RETIREMENT RULE. HOOVER WAS NOW, IN EFFECT, DIRECTOR FOR LIFE.

THE PRESIDENT URGED HOOVER TO INITIATE AN ALL-OUT WAR ON THE KU KLUX KLAN, USING THE SAME COINTELPRO TACTICS THAT WERE USED ON THE COMMUNIST PARTY.

WE WILL NOT BE INTIMIDATED BY THE TERRORISTS OF THE KU KLUX KLAN ANY MORE THAN WE WILL BE INTIMIDATED BY THE TERRORISTS OF NORTH VIETNAM.

ON JULY 10, 1964, THE BUREAU OPENED AN OFFICE IN JACKSON, MISSISSIPPI. THE DIRECTOR OFFICIATED AT THE CEREMONY.

BUREAU MOLES AND INFORMANTS INFILTRATED THE KLAN, LEADING TO THE ARREST, IF NOT THE CONVICTION, OF SEVERAL OF ITS MOST VIOLENT MEMBERS.

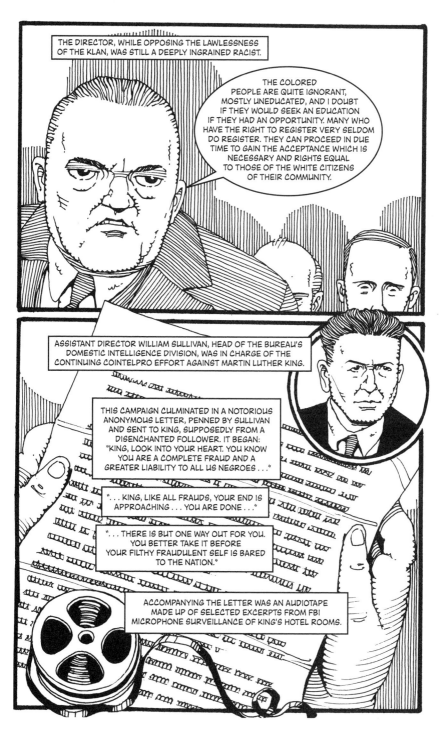

THE DIRECTOR, WHILE OPPOSING THE LAWLESSNESS OF THE KLAN, WAS STILL A DEEPLY INGRAINED RACIST.

THE COLORED PEOPLE ARE QUITE IGNORANT, MOSTLY UNEDUCATED, AND I DOUBT IF THEY WOULD SEEK AN EDUCATION IF THEY HAD AN OPPORTUNITY. MANY WHO HAVE THE RIGHT TO REGISTER VERY SELDOM DO REGISTER. THEY CAN PROCEED IN DUE TIME TO GAIN THE ACCEPTANCE WHICH IS NECESSARY AND RIGHTS EQUAL TO THOSE OF THE WHITE CITIZENS OF THEIR COMMUNITY.

ASSISTANT DIRECTOR WILLIAM SULLIVAN, HEAD OF THE BUREAU'S DOMESTIC INTELLIGENCE DIVISION, WAS IN CHARGE OF THE CONTINUING COINTELPRO EFFORT AGAINST MARTIN LUTHER KING.

THIS CAMPAIGN CULMINATED IN A NOTORIOUS ANONYMOUS LETTER, PENNED BY SULLIVAN AND SENT TO KING, SUPPOSEDLY FROM A DISENCHANTED FOLLOWER. IT BEGAN: "KING, LOOK INTO YOUR HEART. YOU KNOW YOU ARE A COMPLETE FRAUD AND A GREATER LIABILITY TO ALL US NEGROES . . ."

". . . KING, LIKE ALL FRAUDS, YOUR END IS APPROACHING . . . YOU ARE DONE . . ."

". . . THERE IS BUT ONE WAY OUT FOR YOU. YOU BETTER TAKE IT BEFORE YOUR FILTHY FRAUDULENT SELF IS BARED TO THE NATION."

ACCOMPANYING THE LETTER WAS AN AUDIOTAPE MADE UP OF SELECTED EXCERPTS FROM FBI MICROPHONE SURVEILLANCE OF KING'S HOTEL ROOMS.

THE LETTER FAILED TO HAVE ANY EFFECT ON KING'S ACTIVITIES.

IN FACT, HOOVER COULD CONVINCE NO GOVERNMENT AGENCY TO MAKE USE OF THE INFORMATION ON KING.

WHEN, IN APRIL 1968, DR. KING WAS KILLED BY AN ASSASSIN . . . AND TWO MONTHS LATER ROBERT KENNEDY WAS LIKEWISE DISPATCHED, THERE WAS LITTLE MOURNING AT THE FBI.

MEMPHIS, TENNESSEE

LOS ANGELES, CALIFORNIA

THE CONTINUING POLITICAL VIOLENCE OF THE 1960S MADE MANY SUSPECT THAT IT WAS CONTROLLED BY A CENTRAL LEADERSHIP. HENCE A COINTELPRO CAMPAIGN AGAINST BLACK RADICALISM AND LIKEWISE AGAINST THE "NEW LEFT"—THOSE PROTESTING THE DRAFT AND THE ONGOING WAR IN VIETNAM.

U.S. OUT OF VIETNAM

END THE DRAFT

PEACE NOW

THESE GROUPS, TO HOOVER'S MIND, WHILE DOING NOTHING ILLEGAL, WERE NEVERTHELESS DANGEROUS TO THE AMERICAN WAY OF LIFE.

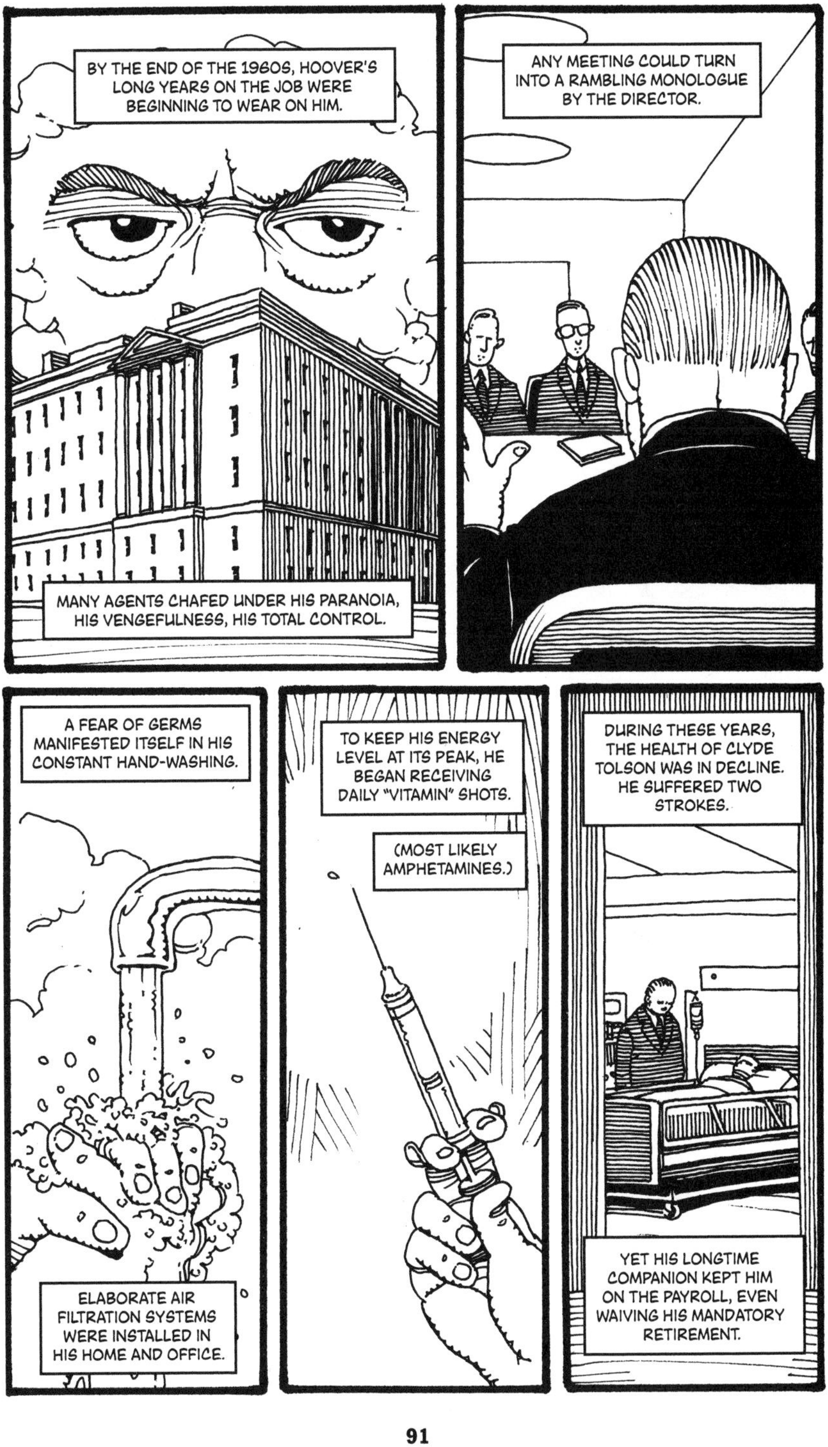
BY THE END OF THE 1960S, HOOVER'S LONG YEARS ON THE JOB WERE BEGINNING TO WEAR ON HIM.
MANY AGENTS CHAFED UNDER HIS PARANOIA, HIS VENGEFULNESS, HIS TOTAL CONTROL.
ANY MEETING COULD TURN INTO A RAMBLING MONOLOGUE BY THE DIRECTOR.
A FEAR OF GERMS MANIFESTED ITSELF IN HIS CONSTANT HAND-WASHING.
ELABORATE AIR FILTRATION SYSTEMS WERE INSTALLED IN HIS HOME AND OFFICE.
TO KEEP HIS ENERGY LEVEL AT ITS PEAK, HE BEGAN RECEIVING DAILY "VITAMIN" SHOTS.
(MOST LIKELY AMPHETAMINES.)
DURING THESE YEARS, THE HEALTH OF CLYDE TOLSON WAS IN DECLINE. HE SUFFERED TWO STROKES.
YET HIS LONGTIME COMPANION KEPT HIM ON THE PAYROLL, EVEN WAIVING HIS MANDATORY RETIREMENT.

PART X
DECLINE AND FALL

IN 1969, RICHARD NIXON BECAME PRESIDENT. HE AND HOOVER HAD BEEN CLOSE ASSOCIATES FOR 20 YEARS.

THE DIRECTOR VIEWED THE INAUGURAL PARADE FROM HIS OFFICE BALCONY . . . AS HE HAD THAT OF EVERY PRESIDENT HE HAD SERVED.

THE NEW ATTORNEY GENERAL, JOHN MITCHELL, WAS A TOUGH LAW-AND-ORDER ADVOCATE VERY MUCH TO HOOVER'S LIKING.

HOOVER AND THE NEW PRESIDENT ALSO SHARED MANY AFFINITIES . . .

. . . CHIEF AMONG THEM THE TENDENCY TO SEE ENEMIES EVERYWHERE.

BUT NIXON'S CLOSEST ADVISERS, BOB HALDEMAN AND JOHN EHRLICHMAN, SHARED NO SUCH CONNECTION.

TO THEM, THE DIRECTOR WAS A LIABILITY, A RELIC, SOMEONE TO BE HUMORED AND EVENTUALLY ELIMINATED.

MANY NEW REVELATIONS ABOUT QUESTIONABLE FBI METHODS, INCLUDING A SERIES BY JACK ANDERSON IN *THE WASHINGTON POST*, ERODED THE BUREAU'S PUBLIC SUPPORT.

SUDDENLY, IT WAS THINKABLE FOR POLITICIANS TO CALL FOR HOOVER'S RETIREMENT.

AS PROTESTS AGAINST THE VIETNAM WAR TURNED EVER MORE VIOLENT, THE NIXON ADMINISTRATION FEARED THAT A FULL-SCALE NATIONAL REVOLT WAS IN THE OFFING.

HOOVER SHARED THE PRESIDENT'S CONTEMPT FOR THE DEMONSTRATORS. ABOUT THE 1970 KILLINGS AT KENT STATE UNIVERSITY, HE ASSERTED . . .

THOSE STUDENTS INVITED AND GOT WHAT THEY DESERVED.

YET TO NIXON'S MEN, HOOVER'S STANCE WAS MORE TALK THAN ACTION.

PEACE

MAK

LOV

NOW

NOT

WAR

HE WAS RELUCTANT TO USE THE FBI'S TRADITIONAL SURVEILLANCE METHODS TO DISRUPT THE ANTIWAR GROUPS.

HOOVER SAW SUCH ACTIVITIES AS POLITICALLY DAMAGING TO THE BUREAU, WHILE THE PRESIDENT HAD NO SUCH SENSITIVITY.

IN 1971, THE DIRECTOR CLOSED DOWN ALL COINTELPRO OPERATIONS.

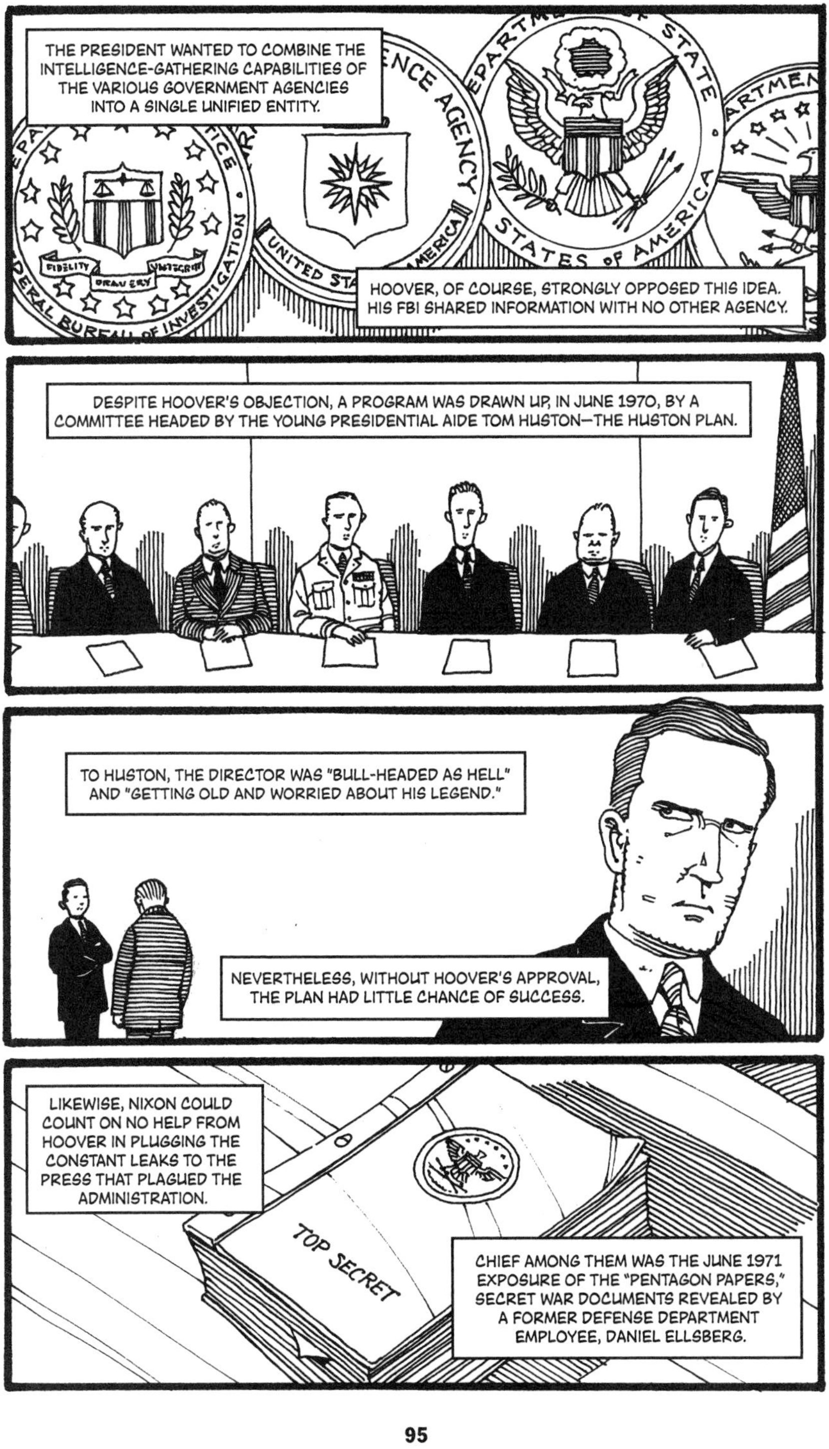
THE PRESIDENT WANTED TO COMBINE THE INTELLIGENCE-GATHERING CAPABILITIES OF THE VARIOUS GOVERNMENT AGENCIES INTO A SINGLE UNIFIED ENTITY.
HOOVER, OF COURSE, STRONGLY OPPOSED THIS IDEA. HIS FBI SHARED INFORMATION WITH NO OTHER AGENCY.
DESPITE HOOVER'S OBJECTION, A PROGRAM WAS DRAWN UP, IN JUNE 1970, BY A COMMITTEE HEADED BY THE YOUNG PRESIDENTIAL AIDE TOM HUSTON—THE HUSTON PLAN.
TO HUSTON, THE DIRECTOR WAS "BULL-HEADED AS HELL" AND "GETTING OLD AND WORRIED ABOUT HIS LEGEND."
NEVERTHELESS, WITHOUT HOOVER'S APPROVAL, THE PLAN HAD LITTLE CHANCE OF SUCCESS.
LIKEWISE, NIXON COULD COUNT ON NO HELP FROM HOOVER IN PLUGGING THE CONSTANT LEAKS TO THE PRESS THAT PLAGUED THE ADMINISTRATION.
TOP SECRET
CHIEF AMONG THEM WAS THE JUNE 1971 EXPOSURE OF THE "PENTAGON PAPERS," SECRET WAR DOCUMENTS REVEALED BY A FORMER DEFENSE DEPARTMENT EMPLOYEE, DANIEL ELLSBERG.

IN FRUSTRATION, NIXON FORMED HIS OWN UNIT TO CONFRONT THE LEAK PROBLEM, THE "PLUMBERS," AS THEY CAME TO BE CALLED.

THEIR MOST NOTORIOUS EXPLOIT WAS A BREAK-IN AT THE OFFICE OF ELLSBERG'S PSYCHIATRIST.

THE PLUMBERS FORMED THE NUCLEUS OF A WHITE HOUSE INTELLIGENCE-GATHERING OPERATION THAT WOULD CULMINATE IN THE 1972 BURGLARY OF DEMOCRATIC CAMPAIGN OFFICES IN THE WATERGATE COMPLEX . . .

. . . LEADING, IN TWO YEARS' TIME, TO THE RESIGNATION OF THE PRESIDENT.

IN THE MEANTIME, NIXON AND HIS MEN SAW NOTHING BUT HARM IN HOOVER'S CONTINUED SERVICE.

IN OCTOBER 1971, NIXON INVITED THE DIRECTOR TO A PRIVATE MEETING IN THE OVAL OFFICE . . .

. . . BUT HOOVER COULD NOT BE PERSUADED TO RESIGN, AND NIXON WOULD NOT FIRE HIM.

SO THINGS REMAINED AS THEY WERE.

ON JANUARY 1, 1972, J. EDGAR HOOVER TURNED 77.

HE WAS AN ISOLATED FIGURE IN THE NEW WASHINGTON, INCREASINGLY ANACHRONISTIC AND OUT-OF-TOUCH.

THE HEROIC BATTLES HE HAD FOUGHT WERE NOW LARGELY FORGOTTEN.

HIS LONGTIME SECRETARY, HELEN GANDY, ON MORE THAN ONE OCCASION FOUND HIM WEEPING LIKE A BABY.

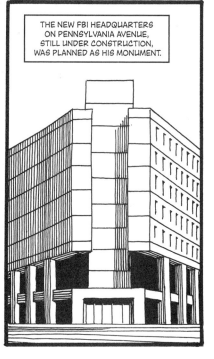

THE NEW FBI HEADQUARTERS ON PENNSYLVANIA AVENUE, STILL UNDER CONSTRUCTION, WAS PLANNED AS HIS MONUMENT.

ON MAY 1, 1972, HOOVER SPENT A FULL DAY AT WORK, LEAVING THE OFFICE AT 6:00 P.M.

HE HAD DINNER AT THE HOME OF THE AILING TOLSON.

BACK HOME AT 10:30, HE GAVE HIS TWO CAIRN TERRIERS, CINDY AND G-BOY, A RUN IN THE BACKYARD.

HE THEN WENT UP TO BED.

THE NEXT MORNING, HOOVER'S COOK AND HOUSEKEEPER, ANNIE FIELDS, BECAME WORRIED WHEN HE WASN'T DOWN FOR BREAKFAST AT HIS USUAL HOUR OF 7:30.

THE FORMER CHAUFFEUR JAMES CRAWFORD WAS SUMMONED TO CHECK THE BEDROOM . . .

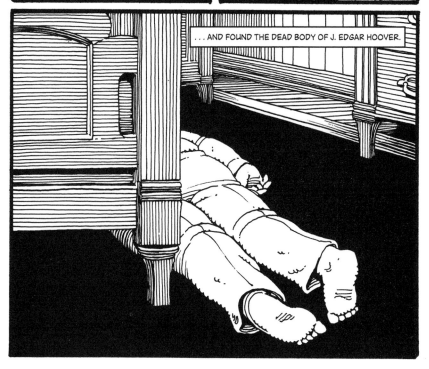

. . . AND FOUND THE DEAD BODY OF J. EDGAR HOOVER.

THE OFFICIAL CAUSE OF DEATH WAS HEART FAILURE, MOST LIKELY BROUGHT ON BY HIGH BLOOD PRESSURE, ALTHOUGH HOOVER'S PERSONAL PHYSICIAN, ROBERT CHOISSER, HAD GIVEN THE DIRECTOR A CLEAN BILL OF HEALTH ONLY MONTHS BEFORE.

IN ANY CASE, NO AUTOPSY WAS PERFORMED.

ON MAY 2 AND 3, AS TRIBUTES POURED IN FROM AROUND THE WORLD . . .

. . . CLYDE TOLSON AND HELEN GANDY DESTROYED ALL THE DIRECTOR'S FILES MARKED "PERSONAL AND CONFIDENTIAL."

HIS REMAINS LAY OVERNIGHT AT GAWLER'S FUNERAL HOME ON WISCONSIN AVENUE.

AT FIRST, HE WAS DISPLAYED IN AN OPEN COFFIN . . .

. . . BUT TOLSON QUICKLY ORDERED IT CLOSED.

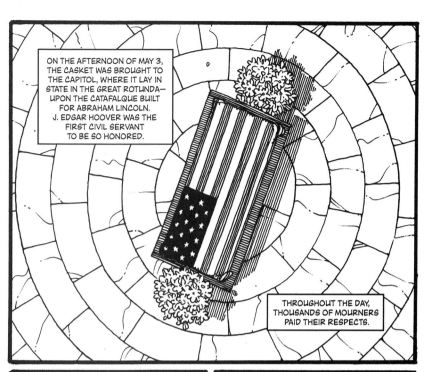

ON THE AFTERNOON OF MAY 3, THE CASKET WAS BROUGHT TO THE CAPITOL, WHERE IT LAY IN STATE IN THE GREAT ROTUNDA—UPON THE CATAFALQUE BUILT FOR ABRAHAM LINCOLN. J. EDGAR HOOVER WAS THE FIRST CIVIL SERVANT TO BE SO HONORED.

THROUGHOUT THE DAY, THOUSANDS OF MOURNERS PAID THEIR RESPECTS.

ON MAY 4, A SERVICE WAS HELD AT THE NATIONAL PRESBYTERIAN CHURCH.

THE PRESIDENT SPOKE THE EULOGY.

THE GOOD THAT J. EDGAR HOOVER HAS DONE WILL NOT DIE. THE PROFOUND PRINCIPLES OF RESPECT FOR LAW, ORDER, AND JUSTICE WILL COME TO GOVERN OUR NATIONAL LIFE MORE COMPLETELY THAN EVER BEFORE.

THE COFFIN WAS THEN TRANSPORTED TO THE CONGRESSIONAL CEMETERY IN SOUTHEAST WASHINGTON.

PENNSYLVANIA AV

J. EDGAR HOOVER WAS LAID TO REST BESIDE HIS MOTHER, HIS FATHER, AND HIS SISTER.

HOOVER

DICKERSON N. HOOVER
1856 ---- 1921

ANNIE M. HIS WIFE
1860 ---- 1938

SADIE MARGUERITE
1890 ---- 1893

JOHN EDGAR HOOVER
1895 ---- 1972

TOLSON DIED IN 1975. HIS GRAVE IS NEARBY.

CLYDE ANDERSON
TOLSON

FURTHER READING

Gentry, Curt. *J. Edgar Hoover: The Man and the Secrets.* New York: Plume, 1991.

Kennedy, David M. *Freedom from Fear: The American People in Depression and War, 1929–1945.* New York: Oxford University Press, 1999.

Patterson, James T. *Grand Expectations: The United States, 1945–1974.* New York: Oxford University Press, 1996.

Powers, Richard Gid. *Secrecy and Power: The Life of J. Edgar Hoover.* New York: Free Press, 1986.

Summers, Anthony. *Official and Confidential: The Secret Life of J. Edgar Hoover.* New York: Putnam, 1993.

Theoharis, Athan G., and John Stuart Cox. *The Boss: J. Edgar Hoover and the Great American Inquisition.* Philadelphia: Temple University Press, 1988.

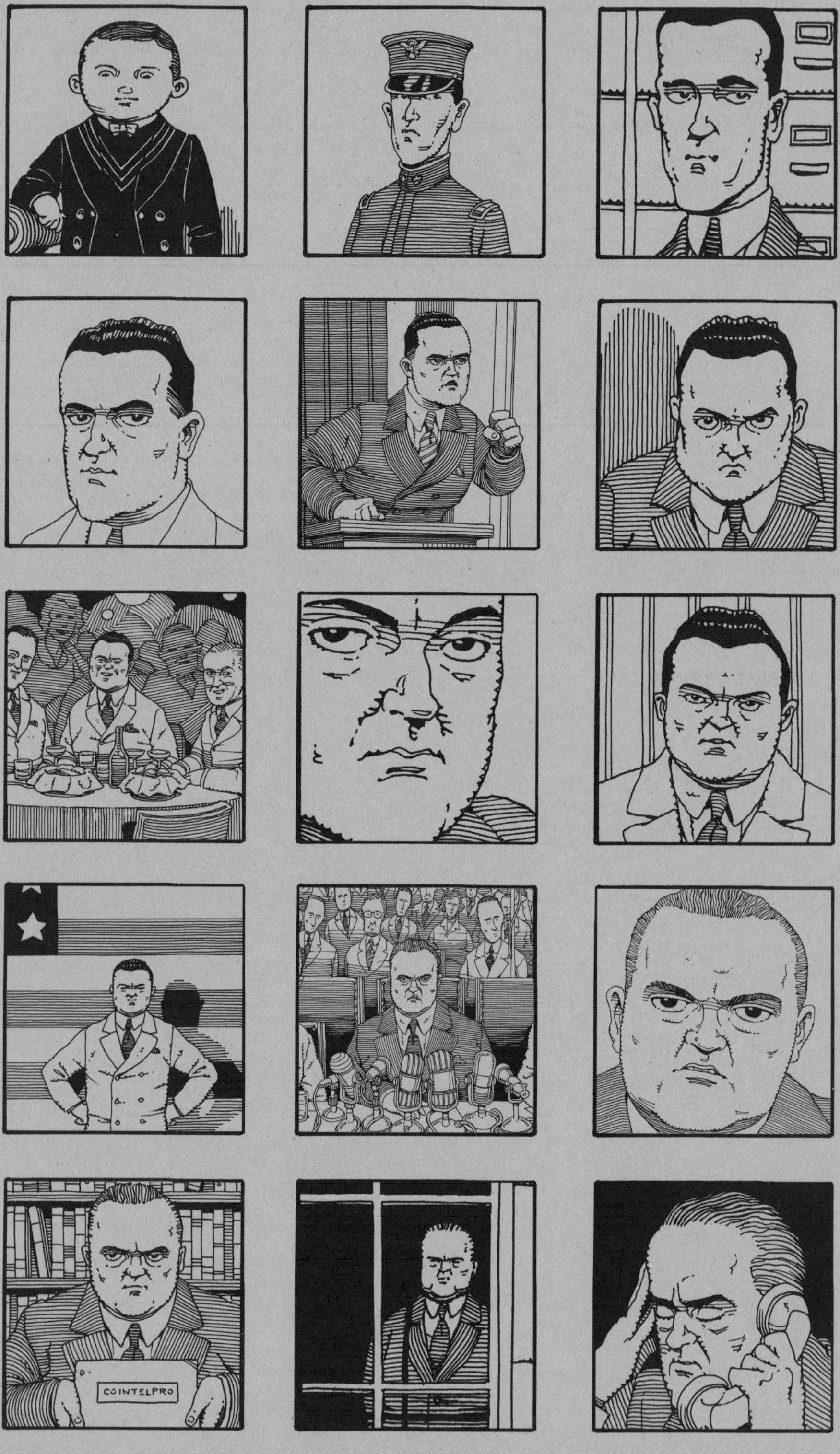
COINTELPRO